CONTE NTS

INTRO

FORE WORD

By Rutger Middendorp

This book was created in a very unorthodox way. I was teaching at the Academy for Pop Culture (Leeuwarden, The Netherlands) and realised there was no great book about concept development for artists. So, I figured I would write one myself. But every time I started, I would wander off into other subjects. There was so much that I wanted our students to know that wasn't covered in the textbooks. Practical stuff like how to pitch your story, find clients, expand a network. It was good stuff—important stuff—but it lacked a common thread.

I shared what I had written with some other art school teachers for feedback. One of them saw an immediate application for it, and used some of the material in a European project on Entrepreneurial Learning. I was asked to join the project and to develop the work I'd already started into a book on entrepreneurial learning. As the idea sharpened, more had to be written, more had to be scrapped, and finally the book got a sense of purpose.

It improved because of input from all the teachers in the project. Contributors from Sweden, Spain, Finland and the Netherlands interviewed artists and added their wise and inspiring quotes. All's well that ends well, I thought at this point.

Then, during one meeting, we decided a book might not be the best form to get this material across. So we made a deck of cards based on the material in the book, which could also exist without it. They say "kill your darlings". The book I originally had in mind is now a dead darling. In its place, we had room to create the creative and comprehensive guide book and cards you now have. If you're looking for some group or solo activities, you can start with the cards and the book can offer further insight and examples. It's a guide where you can look up topics and get more details. Or, if you hate games and love books, it's a resource that you can read and spend time with on its own.

In the end, the book I wanted to write evolved into something that has very little to do with concept development, and instead will help you with the practical, economic and life skills stuff you might not have learned at art school. This book brings in real-world information and insight that make it a pleasure to read. It has some of my own personal experiences together with advice and anecdotes from many other professionals. And I believe it has character and personality, which to me is the most important thing about any book aside from a dictionary.

Thanks to the editor Katherine Oktober Matthews, who ruthlessly edited out a lot of noise, but left enough room for that personality. Lots of people were involved with this project, but there is one person that was absolutely, undoubtedly indispensable: Rebecca Simons. She rallied the troops, organised what needed to be organised and kept me on my toes. Thanks a million.

I hope you enjoy reading this. Feel free to drop me a line at info@rutgermiddendorp.nl Good luck in your creative endeavours. Be nice!

WHY TH IS FIELD GUIDE?

Introduction

Art school can be a pretty amazing place. You are free to create work that you believe is worthwhile. You are surrounded by teachers who help you move forward and by students who you can look up to and cooperate with. You are encouraged to explore, develop and push yourself. But, you can't stay in art school forever.

There will come a time for you to leave this warm, creative nest and come face to face with a much more confusing and cold reality—namely, THE WORLD. You will have to find ways to make money to support yourself, to woo curators or publishers, and to win over customers. Where art school was all about you and your work, everything that comes after will be about you and the world and the relationship between the two. Are you ready for it?

Working as an artist means that it's more likely you will be self-employed, whether as a freelancer or as a business owner. Nearly half of all artists in Europe are self-employed (including visual artists, musicians, dancers, actors and film directors, writers, etc.) This is much higher than the average of the overall working population (15%). Still, many artists graduating from art school feel that they don't have the necessary tools and knowledge to provide for themselves.

Some art schools provide courses on how to start your business, offer internships, invite guest artists to share their experiences, or create connections with the outside world through collaborative projects. But the business side of art almost always remains the painful necessary 'other' for creatives.

---

[1] According to Eurostat (2017)

[2] Based on survey with former art students in Europe conducted by EI-Art

To find new ways of integrating entrepreneurial learning into art schools in a more interesting and accessible way, Rebecca Simons, together with the Finnish school Yrkesakademin i Österbotten, started EI-Art (Entrepreneurial Learning for Artists) in 2011, a collaborative project between art schools in Europe. We started with trainings for students on how to set up, execute and market projects, and then grew to a strategic partnership between six schools from Finland, the Netherlands, Sweden and Spain, to create teaching material on entrepreneurship for creatives.

We believe that many of the key skills and attitudes needed as an entrepreneur are the same ones you already possess as an artist, like creativity, drive and commitment. We also believe that 'networking' and 'promotion' don't have to be dirty words, but can become a natural part of the artistic process. Likewise, 'money' and 'security' are nothing to sneer at, but form the foundation to your practice.

With this material, consisting of a field guide, a set of cards and a website, we aim to lay out for you the key skills, attitudes and knowledge that you will need as an a self-employed artist, AKA a "creative entrepreneur". Whether you aim to have a day job on the side or engage full-time with your art, this material is meant for you. We realise that being a creative entrepreneur means using your creativity and talent to find your own way, so what you won't find here is a book of supposed solutions or an well-worn path to follow. Rather, this material is meant to inspire and empower you to use your creative talents to channel your inner entrepreneur.

Good luck on your journey and let us know if you find your way or if you get stuck. Any questions, feedback or criticism that will help us improve the material is welcome. Drop us a note at www.el-art.org.

Rebecca Simons & the EI-Art team

HOW TO USE THIS MATERIAL

Introduction

The publication *Creativity as a Career: The Field Guide for Artists* consists of a book and a deck of cards and instructions. The full material can be downloaded for free at: el-art.org. This material has been developed to help strengthen the entrepreneurial side of artists (to be). It can be used by art teachers, students, and starting artists. It is suitable for group activities in a classroom setting or informally with peers, but can also just be explored individually in your own home.

The Field Guide
The field guide is the backbone of this material. The text consists of tips, anecdotes, practical assignments and quotes by artists and experts. Its goal is to ask you to think hard about the topics and questions you'll face on your journey of becoming a creative entrepreneur. The field guide is divided into two main sections: YOU and THE WORLD. 'You' is focused on the inner skills you will need to become a creative entrepreneur. 'The World' focuses on the external aspects you'll need to come to grips with as a creative entrepreneur. Each section has four chapters and each chapter includes several topics (see the diagram on page 07). You can read the whole field guide from cover to cover, or just flip to the chapter you need the most at any moment. While using the cards, you can also use the field guide as a reference to get a better understanding of a topic, chapter or section. The field guide is available in full on our website: you can download and print specific topics or you can simply 'print all' to get everything at once. If you prefer to read it in a more traditional book format, you can also order a bound copy of the field guide through print-on-demand.

The Cards

The cards are based on the topics of the field guide and come in three types: Action cards, Question cards and Statement cards. There are also Instruction cards, which suggest ways in which you can use the cards—such as discussions, debates or brainstorms—but you're also free to pick cards at random and freestyle it.

Action cards are practical activities that give you little "push-ups" to do, in order to become a strong creative entrepreneur. Most of the actions can be done within an hour, and some can be done within just a minute. For others, you might feel the need to really work through it with a week-long assignment, or to repeat it for emphasis.

Question cards ask you look for your own truths and answers. You can use these to get to know yourself and other creatives better.

Statement cards present quotes from respected creatives and other (in)famous people, both living and dead, from all kinds of industries. They are meant to challenge your perspective and can be used as a starting point for debate or inner dialogue.

You'll also find blank cards, where you can fill in your own actions, questions, statements or instructions.

Individual use (student/creative)

Creativity as a Career (field guide and cards) will help you on your path to becoming a creative entrepreneur by presenting you with topics you'll encounter when out in the field. It's all about helping you, as an individual, grow stronger and better prepared for your role. As you start to engage with the material, you'll see that being a creative entrepreneur doesn't require a totally new skillset, it's about applying the skills you already have in new ways in order to build the future you want.

One way to start this journey is by defining success on your own terms. You have to know your goal before you know which road to take. This isn't just about your working life, or your business, but your whole (creative) life. So, start with the prologue and pull out the cards on 'The Idea of Success'. Challenge yourself with the Question cards, do the Action cards, and look for inspiration in the Statement cards. Then, once you know what you want to achieve, you can start to figure out how to get there. You can pick and choose topics from the field guide and cards, or, if you're not quite sure where to start, you can download the full field guide and cards and follow it from beginning to end. Or, surprise yourself by picking random cards as a starting point.

This is not a book to be read once and then put on a shelf (or in the bin). As your journey progresses, so will your thoughts. So, we encourage you to write down your thoughts during the process and document the result of your exercises. Revisit the material regularly, maybe annually, to see how you relate to it then. Give yourself the freedom to rewrite your vision of success, to change priorities, and to adapt. Treat this book as the Lonely Planet to your career path: it offers some tips from more seasoned creative travellers to help you find your way, but ultimately it's up to you to make the experience what you want it to be. Now, it's time to set the course for your ideal journey.

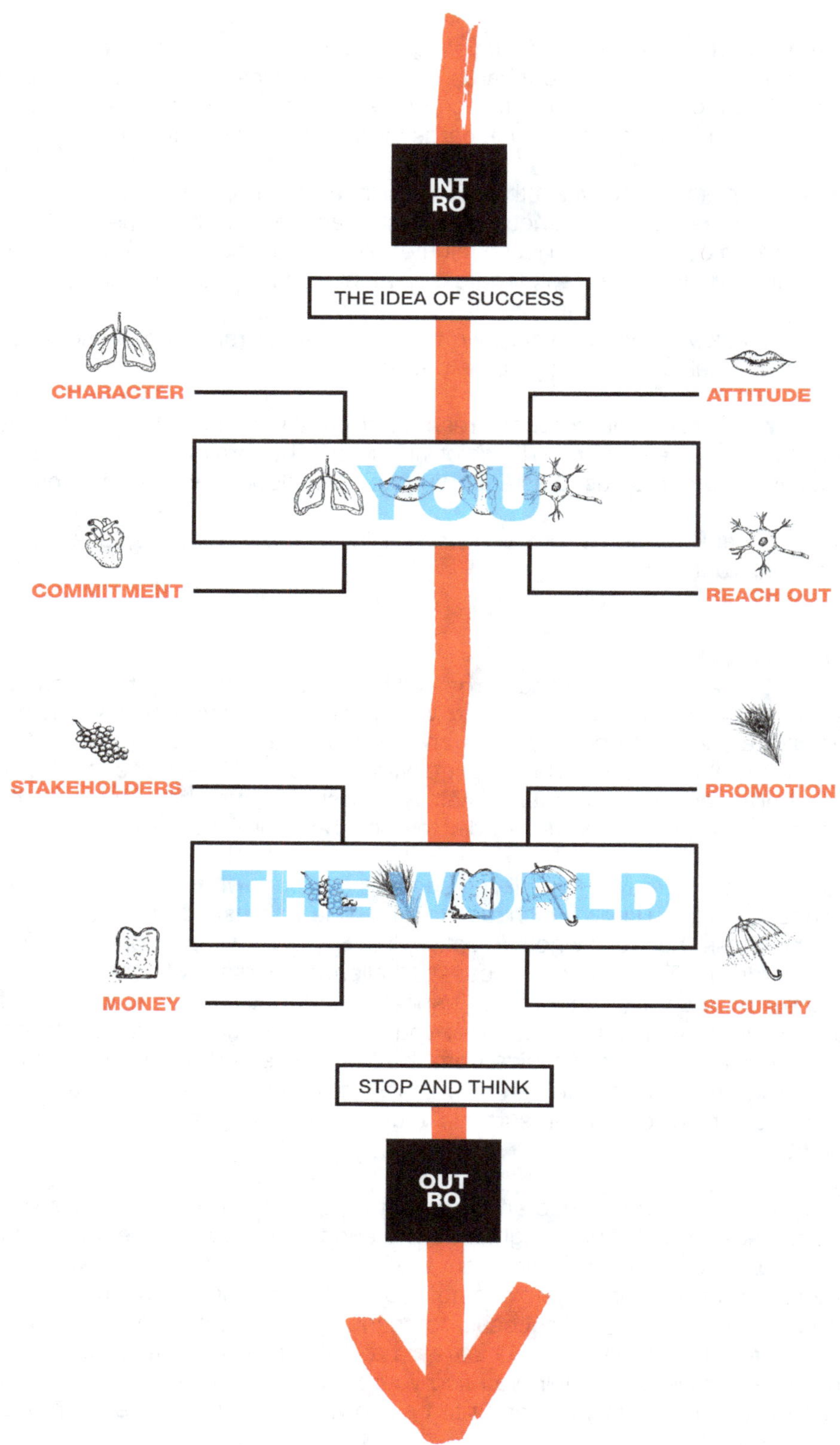
INT
RO
THE IDEA OF SUCCESS
CHARACTER
ATTITUDE
YOU
COMMITMENT
REACH OUT
STAKEHOLDERS
PROMOTION
THE WORLD
MONEY
SECURITY
STOP AND THINK
OUT
RO

Use with groups (teachers / creative groups)

Creativity as a Career (field guide and cards) can be used together as a group to encourage and challenge each other to find your individual ways as (future) creative entrepreneurs. You can spark creative discussion, get to know each other better and find out how you can support and complement each other. You might even find new ways of working together. You can use the cards to ask each other questions, find debate topics in the statements, or try out the exercises together and compare the outcome. See the instructions cards for various ways to use the cards.

Teachers' use

With this material you can help your students become stronger creative entrepreneurs. You can integrate it into your lesson plan as a recurring element or use it within a workshop or other freestanding activities. The material is suitable for secondary level art students up to university students and starting professionals. As a teacher, you can lead the conversation in a way that's appropriate to the level you teach. You can decide whether to just introduce your students to the topics or if you want to do deep work on some sections. The material is also suited for the students to play around with on their own, or an excellent tool to hand to a substitute teacher in your absence. You can use it for an hour or a full week of fun. The material is divided into chapters and sections, so it's also ideal for dividing the material into lessons so that you can revisit it regularly with your students.

The Question and Statement cards are ideal for triggering conversation, and the Action cards can be used both as activities or in discussion: if you don't have time to actually do the actions, you can offer them as hypothetical exercises, where you simply discuss the possible solutions. Many of them can be done within an hour, but you can also choose to extend the time spent on it, by drilling down, or offering assignments that encourage further thought or development.

Pick and choose the topics you want your students to engage with based on their needs, or follow the structure of the guide (see the diagram above). You can also surprise yourself and your students by picking a random card as a starting point. The text from the field guide can be used to introduce the topics to your class first, or assigned as study material afterwards, but you can also jump straight into playing with the various cards and use the guide to look things up as you go. The Instruction cards are there to offer you inspiration on how to use cards in group activities, and you can also come up with your own ideas—the sky's the limit! Remember that this material is not meant to give set answers or pave out a general path, it's meant to spark conversation and inspire students to find their inner entrepreneur and their own preferred journey.

Have fun and contact us with any feedback or suggestions online at: el-art.org

THE IDEA OF SUCCESS

Prologue

What is success? What does it mean to be successful? The meaning most often given to us by mass media and society seems not to have changed much over time: Success is to be powerful, sexy, beautiful, rich, self-driven, independent and assertive. We rarely hear stories about a hero who found a nice balance between work and family, or someone who sacrificed some tokens of success for a little more comfort. And yet, success isn't one-size-fits-all. Depending on your priorities, success has many different shapes.

Take for example this story of a teacher who was also a good writer. He had some poems published, but never hit the big time for his work as a poet, and was never able to spend the time necessary to spread his work more widely. He said: "I have accepted that my talent has not found one big stage, it has been shared among many of my students in small bits. I have peace with the idea that my talent might lead to something big, without the recognition."

You might call that failure, you might call that triumph. Depends on your idea of success.

It turns out, the environment in which you're raised may have a pretty big influence. In the U.S., the famous 'American Dream', which promises that anyone who works hard can achieve greatness, is still alive and well. Take an Uber in LA, and your driver will surely tell you about the script he's working on, the band she's singing in, or the audition that's coming up.

By contrast, there are also environments where striving for success is frowned upon. In Scandinavia, it was put into words wonderfully by Aksel Sandemose in the Law of Jante. The ten rules he wrote include: "You're not to think you are anything special" and "You're not to think you are good at anything." Such an atmosphere makes it pretty challenging to reach for something better.

Consider how you were raised. What beliefs do you hold about success?

FOR EXAMPLE, IS YOUR IDEA OF SUCCESS:

• about excelling, rather than balance?

• about money, rather than contentment?

• about fame, rather than respect?

• about acknowledgment, rather than self-worth?

What is most important is that don't spend your time trying to live up to expectations that are not your own; define your success based on your own values and your true intentions. Find a balance between your short term and long term goals.

Before you dig into this material (guide and cards), find for yourself a clear idea of what you want success to be. It is absolutely essential to know what you want and what your priorities are before charging ahead. It's a lot easier to hit a target when you know what you're aiming for.

HERE ARE SOME WAYS TO FIGURE OUT YOUR IDEA OF SUCCESS. TAKE YOUR TIME FOR THIS, AS IT WILL DEFINE THE REST OF YOUR JOURNEY:
A. Imagine yourself ten years from now. Write down your ideal scenario (success) vs. your doom scenario (failure). What can you compromise and still consider the outcome a success? What boundaries will you not cross? What sacrifices / benefits come with the success?
B. In a group of people, answer the question above individually and then discuss / debate the idea of success together.
C. Do the 'heaven or hell' exercise in the cards - see the instructions.
Also, keep in mind that your idea of success will probably change throughout your life, so continue to revisit this exercise every year.

"I can live off of music, I don't do anything else. That is my success. Once a week I realize I'm a lucky bastard."

**CT Heida,
Musician, The Netherlands**

"To be successful you have to be very clear what you want and what you want your life to look like."

**Yukiko Kitahara,
Ceramist and Founder
Kúu Workshop,
Japan / Spain**

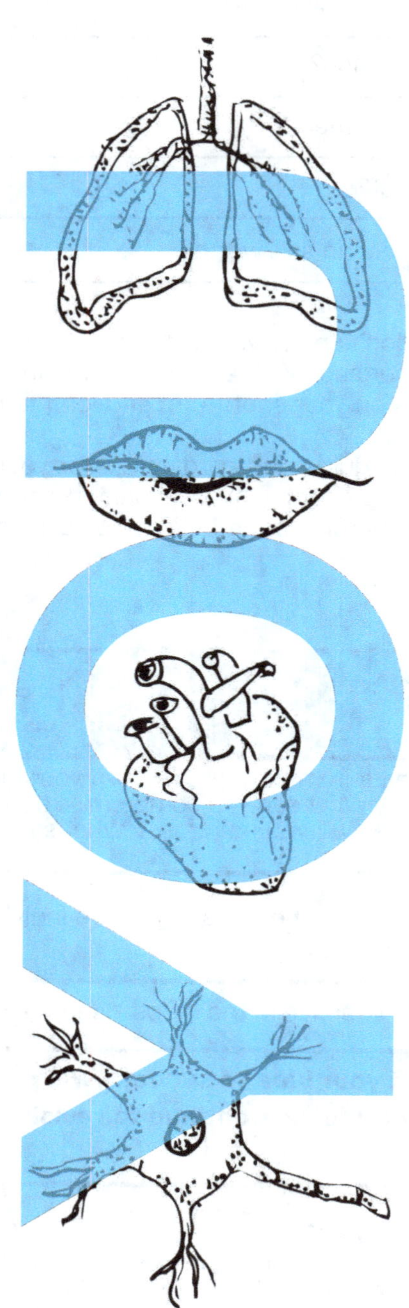

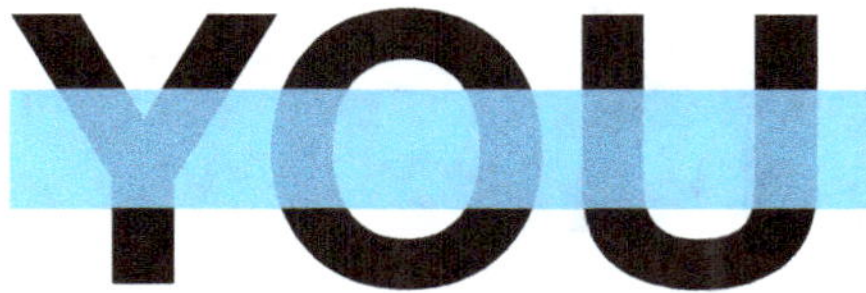

YOU

Who are you? Well, if you're reading this, then you're probably a creative of some kind, whether a musician, visual artist, designer, dancer, theatre maker, writer, etc. There are many reasons why you might've chosen the creative field. Maybe it was based on a gut feeling, maybe someone pointed out that you were talented, or perhaps you just thought it would be fun. And being a creative is fun. Not to mention a rewarding way to bring work into your life.

But be warned, making a living as a creative is hard work. Talent is just your starting point, and luck comes and goes. Your success lies in your own hands. In order to make a living as a creative in today's world, you will need entrepreneurial skills. You will need to become a creative + entrepreneur, a Creative Entrepreneur.

The good news is that the most essential skills for becoming an entrepreneur are pretty common for creative people: curiosity, ambition, a willingness to take risks, problem-solving, and, of course... creativity. Beyond that, you will naturally encounter some aspects of entrepreneurship that aren't familiar to you, that you'll need to develop. That's great! By learning where our weak spots are, we can strengthen them. You might want to start by scanning the Table of Contents for chapters that may need extra attention.

Let's start by establishing now that the new **YOU** is no longer just 'a creative' but a Creative Entrepreneur. This field guide and deck of cards will help you to embrace and develop your entrepreneurial side.

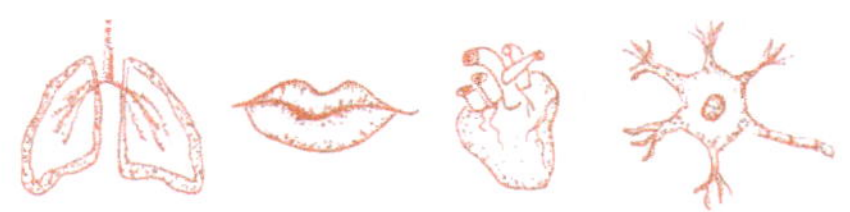

CHAR ACTER

Character is the quality that makes you who you are, but that doesn't mean it's set in stone. You can work on forming your character, making your strengths stronger. Being talented is a great gift, but also just a seed if you don't nurture it. If you can learn to see your talent and your creativity as just a starting point, it will help you look for paths that will take you further. Your goals can only be reached through developing your character traits; it will require persistence as well as having a strategy.

Being a creative entrepreneur is a two-way street: you will need to send things out into the world, and also be prepared for what the world throws back at you. So, communication is a skill you need to practise. Not everyone is outgoing naturally, but you can learn how to better communicate with your audience and clients. As for what the world throws at you, it's all about perspective. Critical feedback can be a great learning tool; if you can condition yourself to handle it the right way, it will help strengthen your character as well as your art.

CREATIVITY AS A BUSINESS TOOL

Character

If you choose an artistic profession, chances are you're pretty creative (or a gifted craftsman). But, do you also think of ways to apply that creativity beyond your work, into the running of your artistic business? Creativity is key to entrepreneurship, too. It can for example be used to find novel ways to reach a target audience and to solve time and budget constraints.

How can you use your creativity to make a living as an artist? By using the same technique that you (knowingly or unknowingly) use to make art.

**Start off with a nice and narrow question, for example:
How can I make money with my art?**

Step 1: Fill a shoebox with the most wonderful ideas of making money you can find. There are some nice examples in this book, but be sure to add some of your own.

Step 2: Expand on the ideas. How could you improve them?
Can you combine two or more? Can you adapt them to better fit your work?

Step 3: Gloss through all the ideas. Sort them in any way you see fit.

Step 4: Sleep on it. Forget about it. Get away. Give your head some time to process all the ideas that you've given it.

Step 5: Return to your sorted ideas. You will know which one to use. If not, return to Step 1.

See, it's easy to apply the basic steps of the creative process to get you going as an entrepreneur.

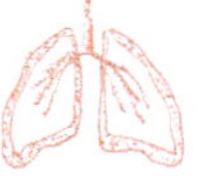

"To keep creative, the most important thing is the desire to always learn and not settle for what you already know."

Francisco Alcántara, Architect and Musician, Spain

TALENT VS. PERSEVERANCE VS. STRATEGY

"Hard work beats talent if talent doesn't work hard."
—Tim Notke, high school basketball coach, USA

Talent is highly overrated. If you stop and think about it, it's absolutely clear that the most talented people in the world are not necessarily the most successful ones. And more importantly, the most successful ones aren't the most talented.

If you've ever heard a live performance by Madonna, or another megastar, you know it's not all about having the best voice. The same goes for most jobs. We don't live in a meritocracy. At least, not the way you think. You need a lot more than talent to succeed. For starters, you'll need talent, perseverance and strategy. This chapter elaborates on this holy trinity.

Let's start with talent, 'cause that part is short and sweet. You were born with certain talents. But that raw talent is just the seed; it won't grow unless you nurture it. You've got to develop your talent for it to be worth anything. So, get to work.

This brings us to perseverance. Perseverance is all about putting in the work. No matter what you're trying to learn, trial and error is a necessary part of the process. Whether you're learning to walk, play an instrument, or design a website, the ability to persevere through failure is a must. It's better in all these instances to realise that you're in the process of learning, and not get so caught up with the current result. The same is true for starting a business. Most entrepreneurs that we now think of as successful talk about the many failures on their path to getting there. As the American inventor Thomas Edison put it: "Genius is one percent inspiration, ninety-nine percent perspiration." So get out there and sweat! Perseverance is key to success.

The third part of the holy trinity of success is strategy. Simply put: how do I go about things? If your goal is to become wildly popular with your work, how do you put your talents and hard work into action to achieve that goal? There are all kinds of strategic decisions to be made in production, for example by choosing materials that are inexpensive or luxurious, as well as in sales and marketing, such as in setting your price point and deciding how and where to promote your work.

If you want to make a living with your art, you'll need to have talent, the grit to persevere through hard times, and a good strategy to carry it out.

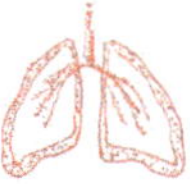

"Nothing happens overnight. It's not one moment of glory, it's a gradual process. Every step of the way is important."

**Melissa Henderson,
Visual Artist, Sweden**

SPEAK UP

An outgoing personality can absolutely come in handy when you want to get your career moving, but not all of us are comfortable being the life of the party. For some, talking about yourself and your work is downright unpleasant. Well, there are other ways to get noticed, but sooner or later, you'll have to be able to express yourself verbally. Start by challenging yourself to talk about your work and practise your pitch. It's all about confidence, and if you don't have it you can build it.

First, realise you have something to say. No matter what kind of creative work you're doing, whether visual art, music or otherwise, there is meaning and personality in your work that deserves to be heard. Also, nobody knows your story better than you, so start believing in the power of telling your own perspective.

Next, start tailoring your talk to your audience. Depending on who you are talking to, you might want to change your tone and style, so imagine you are presenting your work to people of different profiles and how you'd need to adjust your message for each of them. For example, start with people you are comfortable with, like your neighbour, your fellow students, your friends. Then, move on to people you don't know, or who intimidate you. The key is to be able to explain the core of your story in a way that is suitable for the person(s) listening. Why is it relevant for them? How do you engage them in your story?

From here, you'll be able to work on your delivery. Make a video recording of yourself speaking to see how it comes across to other people. Pay attention, for example, to how often you say "um", how you use your hands and what your body language is saying.

Then, practise till you're comfortable. Public speaking is often ranked as people's number one fear, so just remember that being afraid is a perfectly normal reaction. A little nervousness will turn into adrenaline and keep you sharp, so embrace it. Your body is trying to help you. But to avoid turning into a nervous wreck, the best thing to do is to practise, practise, practise, ask for feedback and practise some more. This will help you to get truly comfortable, so that you can let go, let your personality shine through and even crack a joke when it's needed. In the end you will be ready to look your audience in the eye and come across as the expert you are.

You can also be heard (and seen) without talking directly to a person, for example on your website and on social media. Make sure you have a presence that reflects the meaning and personality of your work.

You have something to say, so don't mumble (literally nor figuratively). Speak up about your work and yourself.

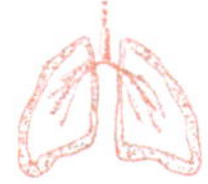

HANDLING CRITICISM

Character

"Other rappers diss me. Say my rhymes are sissy. Why? Why? Why? What? Why exactly? What? Why? Be more constructive with your feedback, please, why?"
—Flight of the Conchords, Comedy Duo, New Zealand

It can be quite daunting to invite criticism, but the ability to handle criticism well is a sign of an evolved human being. If you harness criticism as a tool to make you stronger and better at what you do, you will invite it. Wholeheartedly.

Growing up, most of us learn through encouragement and lessons from our parents and teachers. Hearing only encouragement may help you build confidence but will not necessarily stimulate you to develop yourself and your work, nor will accepting all the lessons from your parent or teacher at face value. It's important to learn to invite feedback and embrace criticism, and to hear it with your own critical ear, rather than take it all in as truth. When it comes to criticism, the one giving it is not necessarily right (or wrong). It is simply a unique new view on your work from a perspective that you yourself can never obtain.

To better invite criticism, first, accept that you do not know everything and that it is impossible to do everything perfectly. Insight on your work from others might very well be helpful.

Second, accept that you are responsible for your own work. No matter what anyone else might say, you have the final decision and responsibility for which feedback you allow to influence your work. Accepting feedback doesn't make your work less 'yours'.

Third, understand that feedback is not about you, but about your work. Observe the feedback neutrally, take notes, and later you can determine which points to adopt and which to reject. Don't justify or explain; rather, use the opportunity to make sure you understand what someone means. Ask to clarify, not to defend.

One day, if you're lucky, a professional critic will review your work—and it may not be good. This is something that you cannot control when you put your work into the public eye, and their words might hit you extra hard when you realise that this criticism will have further reaching implications. This is when it's important to remember that being reviewed is positive in itself. The critic has invested time and energy in your art, and has then published their findings about your work, increasing its visibility and also causing it to be discussed in relation to other works. You don't have to agree with any of it; treat it as an opportunity to better understand the world into which your art fits.

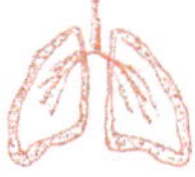

"If you need to make money out of your art you have to consider what other people think."

**Tobias Granbacka,
Pianist, Finlandect, Spain**

ATTIT UDE

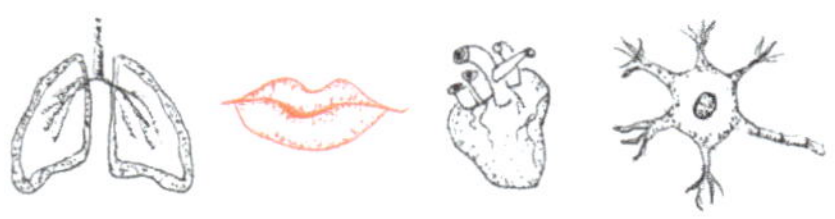

Your attitude is your position, the way you think or feel about something. Being confident and fearless is an attitude that can help you progress, but when pushed too far along the spectrum, switches over to arrogance, which can hold you back. As a creative entrepreneur, you will need to take risks but also to know when the risk is not worth it. You'll need to learn when to say yes and when to say no. In order to survive, you have to be adaptable, but that doesn't mean that you should go wherever the stream takes you. It all comes down to finding the attitude that helps you achieve your own version of success.

CONFIDENCE:

Attitude

BELIEVE YOU WILL SUCCEED

The essence of any creative endeavour is finding a new way to capture/ illustrate/make/do/tell something. It is to explore the unexplored and express the unexpressed. This quest therefore has one preeminent danger: the fear of failure.

The fear of failure can be paralyzing, and unproductive to your creative process. Failing itself, as opposed to the fear of failure, is simply a part of the process. It may feel safer to not challenge yourself or try new things, but the safety of old patterns will not bring you closer to your goal of achieving something unique.

Boost your confidence by challenging yourself to do something that feels a little bit bigger than usual, something a bit scary. Your goal isn't necessarily to avoid failing, but to overcome the fear of failure. Try something that pushes you to be better than you are right now—give yourself a bigger pair of shoes to fill. And if you fall down in your new shoes, simply stand up and try again. The key is confidence in yourself. With practise, you will gain confidence in your ability to pick yourself up after you fall.

Dutch fashion designer and artist Marlies Dekkers says that being a bit arrogant is good when you are young because it keeps your spirit up and moves you forward. She believes that the key to her success was that she was not afraid; she was proud of herself. "If you don't believe in yourself then other people will never believe in you."

Yet, it's also good to look at yourself honestly: remember that you cannot be good at everything. Try to figure out what your strengths are and for what aspects you need to seek assistance or people to collaborate with.

Tell yourself again and again that you will succeed. Or, find other people who will tell you this again and again. Just remember that it's better to try and fail, than to never try at all. In failure you will learn new things, and grow confidence in yourself with each time that you dust yourself off, and try again.

SAY NO!

Attitude

When you've just started working, it seems like every opportunity is one to jump at. You're keen to make more work, to get to know new people. And to prove yourself.

However, at any point in your career, it is important to really evaluate every opportunity you get. You might think that it's better to do a new project than to do nothing at all, but it might not be. Keep in mind that your most valuable assets are your time and attention. If you are in the midst of a project, that's where your time and attention will go, leaving you less open to other incoming opportunities. Saying "no" to a project will help you protect your time and attention, to give them more fully to current projects you've already committed to, or new ones that are better aligned with your goals.

Imagine you are an artist that does photography. You want to make very personal work that resonates with an audience. You are asked to shoot someone's family portrait in front of their house. It will pay your rent for a month and you will have a project on your hands.

This assignment is not your work though. You are not in charge of making something artistic, you have a client with wishes. There is nothing wrong with that, because sometimes we must make choices according to different reasons and needs, it's just important to evaluate what is the cost of taking any assignment that is not the work you want to make. It's also important to recognise the difference between your work and your assignment, when you're building your online portfolio.

So, with any offer for work, ask yourself: does this contribute to reaching my goal? Does this in any way distract me from my goal? Will this project bring me closer to a relevant audience with relevant work? Does this help me build my brand?

Of course, sometimes the more permeating question is, "How will I pay rent this month?" You won't always be in the luxurious position to base your decisions on the question of your artistic goals. When that's the case, just make sure you have a clear understanding in your own mind between 'bread-work' and 'career-work'.

"If you take on everything, maybe in the short term you'll achieve some success, but it's risky because you may end up doing things you regret. Being selective pays off only in the long term, but people will know who you are and what you do."

Salvatore Vitale,
Photographer and Co-founder of YET Magazine, Switzerland

SAY YES!

If you tend to overthink your decisions, worry less about saying "no" and start saying "yes" to opportunities. Every decision will have its pros and cons, and the big upside to a new project is that it multiplies the chances for happy accidents.

When you take on a new project, you'll meet more people, you'll get to do new things, you'll learn more about your field or your industry, and you'll discover qualities about yourself that you didn't even know you had. When you try something a little out of your comfort zone, the best part is the unknown: by pushing yourself, you learn what you're capable of. There is much to be gained when you're open enough to say "yes" to something.

As long as you realise (and make sure) a project is not a one way street, you can feel free to take on new challenges. Be smart about committing to projects that you've got time and energy for, and even better if they're aligned with your goals.

If you're not certain about accepting an offer, try not to focus only on the negative aspects. Instead, focus on everything that the experience will give you.

ASK YOURSELF:

• Will I meet new people?

• Will I get to do new and exciting things?

• Does it offer me an interesting challenge?

• Why not?

• Will my plants and cat survive?

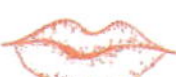

THINK OUTS IDE THE BOX

Attitude

"If the rules are not broken, we will be."
—Yoko Ono, Multimedia artist, singer, songwriter, and peace activist, Japan

English musician and record producer Brian Eno created a set of cards called the Oblique Strategies. It's a way to get even seasoned musicians to rediscover their creativity and take creative risks, for example, telling a guitarist to play with only one hand. Or a tuba player to make sounds with the instrument in an unintended way. Rethinking the things you take for granted, like the 'right' way to play an instrument, leads to unexpected results. In essence, creativity.

As a creative entrepreneur you have two jobs: You are a maker and a business owner. In both capacities you need to take risks to advance. You need to think outside the box in your artistic work, as encouraged by Brian Eno's cards, but also in your approach to your business. Think about how you invest in materials. Re-evaluate the places that you think are the best to work or to show your work. Try closing yourself off from the world for a couple of weeks to truly focus on making something with the potential to make money. By getting out of your patterns of thought and action, and taking risks, you invite bigger and better things.

RUTGER'S FIELD NOTES

I once talked to an entrepreneur who had been a millionaire at least twice and had lost almost everything twice. I told him that I admired his entrepreneurial stamina and his energy to try again, even after losing it all. He said: "There's no way you can win, when there's no way you can lose."

"At the beginning of my career, I had many ideas about what art was and was not, but I have concluded that the most important thing is to be free in your expression. To be free you must gamble and take risks. It's the only way you're going to make interesting work. Don't just sit and sketch the same thing again and again. You have a mission and your only mission is to take risks!"

Jonas Liveröd,
Artist works with Sculpture, Drawing and Installation, Sweden

Attitude ADAPT ABILITY

We've all heard of Darwin's principle of 'survival of the fittest', but it's often misunderstood; it's not the physically strongest animal who will survive, but the one best fit to the environment. The animal that's best adapted to the given circumstances.

The same goes for you as an artist. The better you are at adapting to any given situation—whether that means changing yourself or your situation—the better your chances of 'survival'. When there is a flood, you can build a tower or learn how to live underwater. When digital photography is booming, you can change according to the trend, or make your analogue photography a part of your brand. As long as you don't sit around watching the water rise around you, you will find a way to adapt.

At its root, adaptability is a response to the need to solve a problem. First, you have to define what the 'problem' is. Are you trying to pay the bills? Create innovative work? Trying to find the right direction? Adaptability is not about changing wildly and blindly in response to the world around, but about taking note of what new adaptations help your chances for survival, and what hurts.

So be aware of what's changing, and how it succeeds (or doesn't). Keep your eyes open. Learn about new tech, investigate new ways of reaching an audience and read up on what other artists are doing. Reflect on how it impacts you and your practice, then adapt.

"The world around is continuously changing. At every step of the way, you have a choice to make: decide it's time to be left behind, keep pace, or forge the way forward."

Katherine Oktober Matthews, Artist and Analyst, The Netherlands

COMM ITMENT

Being dedicated to your work as an artist means to fully embrace what you do, taking the good with the bad, and putting in the necessary hours. Yes, being an artist is hard work. However, even doing what you love doesn't mean dedicating your whole life to your art (business). There's still space for having a good work-life balance. You can also learn to work smarter, not harder, to get the most out of your hours. And, taking on a side job doesn't mean that you've sold out; on the contrary, it might be what's needed to pursue your art. It's about finding the right balance and the right fuel to keep going.

Commitment TIME MANAGEMENT

If you really want to make/write/produce something, you need to find the time to do it. It is all too easy to postpone our tasks, since making something creative can be quite a challenge and failure is not a sentiment most of us have learned to embrace. Without a deadline, you may find yourself postponing your work indefinitely. Doing so ensures that your project can't fail, but it also means that it never gets a chance to succeed.

Without a deadline, there is no urgency.
Without urgency, there is no project.

So, start by setting a deadline. And, even better: chop up your work into small, manageable chunks and set deadlines for each. Leave room for failure and exploration. A great way to hold yourself accountable is to tell others about your deadline, so they will ask how it's coming along. Critically, you'll need learn to live by your own deadlines. Take them seriously, and on occasions when you're truly not able to meet them, don't throw away your planning, but reschedule. Afterwards, reflect on how you could've planned better.

"I've figured out three tricks that work for me:

1. In the morning I can work really hard. If I start at 8:00 then I do a lot before 11:00.
2. I have chosen a colour for each project that I'm working on and I use those colours in my digital agenda for each project. Sometimes things come up and you have to change the plan, but then at least I realise that I have to fit those hours somewhere else. It really works.
3. When writing, I put my timer on 40 minutes to just focus. In that time I try to stick to my desk, and not make any calls or grab a coffee."

Iris Sikking,
Independent Curator, The Netherlands

Time management isn't the sexiest subject, but done right it will become second nature. It is about being the master of your time. Nowadays, our lives are filled with ways in which others can distract us and make demands on our time—phone calls, social media messages, emails, etc.—but through time management, you can create blocks of time to focus on your own goals, ensuring that it's you who determines what you do with your day.

Step 1: The Purge
Throughout one week, make an honest list of how you spend your time, in 15 minute chunks. Include the time you spend on your phone, browsing, taking a shower, sleeping, commuting, etc. Look at things that absorb a lot of time, but do not give you much in return, in particular 'downtime' activities like watching tv, gaming or texting. See if you can win some of that time back by imposing some rules on yourself. Try to find the ideal balance, in which your downtime rejuvenates you for your uptime.

Step 2: The Intel
Time management starts with a clear picture of what actually needs to be managed. What are the goals and responsibilities that take up time? Stephen Covey has a great book about setting up an entire system for determining where your time goes, but it's quite intense and not for everybody. You can also use this simple method: Make a list of the different roles you have. For each, define the recurring tasks. Then, add to the list any upcoming one-off tasks.

Step 3: The Overview
Now, make a huge space on your wall to work on your planning, where you can pin pieces of paper or use stickies. Start with your recurring tasks, assigning each one to a specific day in the week. This will give you an idea of how much flexible and free time you have. If you have more tasks than time, try to rid yourself of any time-consuming tasks that do not contribute to your long term goals. Then, add the one-off tasks.

Repeat every week

WORK-LIFE BALANCE

Commitment

There are a lot of decisions you take in life that can have a lasting effect on your work. For example, let's say you're considering living in your parents' basement rent-free. It may cost you some street cred, but will earn you the freedom to spend time on your goals. Or, let's say you're thinking of starting a family. That will cost you a lot of time for your projects, but may earn for you a sense of belonging that deeply inspires you.

How should you make the big decisions that will have a lasting impact on your time and budget? What is the true cost of a rock 'n' roll lifestyle?

Of course, there is no single "right" way to create your life. Every individual will make choices to find her or his own preferred balance. It might even be the case that what you think will bring balance to your work and life, doesn't. A great example is the writer Walter van den Berg, who quit his day job once he was successful enough to live off his books, only to find out that he wasn't able to write without the perspective and distraction that his day job offered to him.

When making the big decisions in life, many will try to offer you advice and wisdom, but ultimately you will have to make the choice work for you. Before taking any big decisions that will be hard to walk away from, be sure to first take an honest look at all the possible ways it may impact your life—both what it gives to you, and what it costs.

"Someone else would say my life is unbalanced, but my life is my work so I think my life is balanced."

Yukiko Kitahara, Ceramist and Founder Kúu Workshop, Japan / Spain

RUTGER'S FIELD NOTES

When I finished university, I found myself in the privileged position to buy a house. Then, three years later, I realised I wanted to pursue a different job. But, if I were to quit my job then and there, I wouldn't be able to afford my house anymore. My choices were interlinked: if I couldn't sell my house, I couldn't quit my job. I was married to the house.

"I'm used to being away, it is a sacred space. I know that I can completely devote myself to what I do. I then quite often work late, whereas when I'm at home I try to avoid that."

Anna-Maria Helsing, Conductor, Finland

"I take my personal life with the same importance as I take a job, so it gets the time it deserves. I force myself to go out with friends and make plans."

Francisco Alcantara, Architect and Musician, Spain

FINANCIAL SECURITY

Commitment

Who is more free: A person who has an okay job, no financial worries, and lots of free time, or, a person who has a dream job, with no financial security and no control over their free time?

The answer will probably differ from one person to the next. How much does the first person like the job, how financially insecure is the second? But the point of the question is to demonstrate that life as a creative does not grant you total freedom. At the very least, you will have to find food and shelter, so there are practical and financial obligations. This is a helpful realisation.

In her book "How to Be an Artist Without Losing Your Mind…" JoAnneh Nagler suggests that the perfect solution is to get a day job. Not a bad suggestion, but it's not necessarily the best one for everybody. Creative people tend to find different ways to cope with their financial responsibilities. Here's a few options:

01. Find a job (that isn't necessarily related to your work, or personally fulfilling) for a couple of days a week that gives you financial stability. This will buy you the time and headspace to do your own work the rest of the time.

02. Find a creative job in the field you like, but in the type of job that is more secure. For example, if you're a musician, get a job at a festival or podium.

03. Reduce financial responsibility as much as you can by aggressively avoiding financial commitments. For example, travel by bike or foot instead of car or public transport, find a vacant house you can housesit instead of paying for accommodation.

Whatever you choose, realise the trade-offs you're making between creative freedom, time and commitment. Find a balance that works for you.

"Try a lot of different things. Have one steady job for your income and do a lot of different things on the side."

**Karin Noeken,
Theatre Director, The
Netherlands**

FIND YOUR FUEL

Commitment

No one is inspired all the time. If being creative is your job, though, you can't just wait for inspiration to strike, you've got to get to work even when the tank is empty. The question is, how? If staring at a blank canvas only gets you more frustrated, look elsewhere for the fuel you need. Here's a few tips that might help you get refuelled, and back on the road.

Inspire yourself with other people's work

To remind yourself why creative work is so worthwhile, it's not a bad start to experience some of the results. Visit a concert of a band you love or maybe one you hate. Go to the theatre and be surprised, annoyed, triggered or shaken. Be a regular at museums, galleries, and gatherings with other artists. You will find new ideas, new energy and fuel for your creative process and your business. Don't be scared to see things a little outside of your comfort zone, whether it's experimental opera, or a local museum you never bothered to visit. You'll be surprised at all the strange places you find fuel. And, just so we're clear: Yes, when you're a creative, going to concerts, plays, movies and exhibitions is actually part of your job.
Cool, huh?

Console yourself with other people's struggles

Sometimes, seeing other people's successful projects can feel demoralising. If it seems like every other artist is succeeding and you're struggling, it's time for a little more perspective: all creatives sometimes struggle, and all creatives sometimes fail. The NPR Podcast "How I Built This", for example, is a series of interviews with entrepreneurs who tell the story of how they became successful. Along the way, they always seem to have 'back against the wall' and 'should I quit?' type moments. It really is part of the process. And though we might think we already know that, it's good to be reminded. Then there's the Netflix documentary series "Abstract", in which successful artists present their work and how they go about it. There are of course happy endings, but also very real struggles and self-doubt. Car designer Ralph Gilles had to be dragged out of the basement by his brother to achieve the success he has today.
Go figure.

"You might feel that you have to be behind your computer for long hours. However, a walk or a visit to an exhibition can spark many new ideas that you don't get while sitting down. I get the best thoughts when travelling therefore I always carry around a small booklet to write down my ideas."

**Iris Sikking,
Independent Curator, The Netherlands**

PUT IN THE WORK

Commitment

The great thing about being a creative entrepreneur is that all the time and effort you invest in your work has a direct benefit for you. The downside is that it all comes down to you, so if you don't put in the work, there is no progress. It's hard work.

So, what does it mean to work hard? First and foremost, it's putting in the hours necessary to build your craft, to constantly learn and improve, to show your work, and to network and meet people. Beyond that, it's working not only hard but smart: being aware of how to use the time you have wisely, make plans, focus on specific goals and take the time to create quality.

At the beginning of your artistic career, it may seem like success is a finish line. However, achieving some measure of success only raises the stakes for your next project, making it all the more important that you are in a constant process of creating opportunities. It helps to remember that while there are of course moments to celebrate, there are no finish lines. You still have to work and evolve to keep your momentum moving forward.

The American illustrator Christoph Niemann said he came to the a wonderful realisation that being inspired was not something he had to wait for, but that if he worked from 9 to 5, inspiration would come at some point. He just had to start working. Whether you are working on a new design, a new song, or a new sculpture, it pays to just start working. It's better to make a shitty thing you can improve on, than to wait for a fully formed idea to pop into your head. That's not likely to happen.

It is a lot easier to put in the work after you realise that every single second you devote to your work makes it better. With every single thing you make, you improve as an artist and as an entrepreneur.

"If I don't work I don't get paid, but it's not only about money, it's about evolving. We are lucky, because of course it's work, but it's not a job."

Salvatore Vitale, Photographer and Co-founder Yet Magazine, Switzerland

"Hard work! It is all about hard work! Work a lot with your instrument or the things you want to improve in your artistry. There are no shortcuts!"

Caroline Leander, Pianist, Singer and Composer, Sweden

"You need to work really hard, I need to work really hard, be prepared to work really hard."

Martin Brandqvist, Musician, Composer & Actor, Sweden

"It mainly comes down to hard work. Even if you have talent, without hard work you're not going anywhere."

Jesús Prudencio, Graphic Designer and Illustrator, Spain

REACH OUT

The artist as a lone wolf is an old romanticised notion. Yes, you probably need some peace and quiet to come up with your ideas, or to bring them to life, but there is also a world out there that you're dependant on. The people around you are your audience, your inspiration, your clients, your network. Your communication with them isn't a broadcast radio, it's an ongoing and complex dialogue. Increased activity leads to opportunity, but before you start reaching out, it's good to consider why and how you want to communicate. What you want to gain from the outside world, and what can you give in return? Will you let the demand steer your output or will you let your work determine your audience? Consider what you want your audience to gain or what kind of impact you want your work to have on the world. Deciding where to live can also be an important part of the equation in positioning yourself and your relationship with the world.

SOLITUDE VS. CONFRON TATION

Reach out

*"I live in that solitude which is painful in youth,
but delicious in the years of maturity."*
—Albert Einstein

Here's an experiment: Try to go a whole day without anyone talking to you. It's pretty hard. Phone calls and texts, emails, social media and advertisements; you are inundated with communication. It's like drinking from a waterfall. And with each of these messages, you are informed of things someone else already came up with. To give your own thoughts a little space to grow and take form, you need peace and quiet. In a 24/7 society, that means you have to protect your space and time. This will help you to resist outside interference. To not fall back on the comfort from other people's presence and reassurance. To be able to listen to, and know yourself.

In the excellent book *A Technique for Producing Ideas*, one of author James Webb Young's key steps is: "Forget about it." That is, after working very actively or intensely on something, it's important to step back from it. Why? Well, scientists have shown that most of our brain activity is unconscious. We simply do not know what's going on up there. The more we try to focus, the more we distract ourselves from listening to our own subconscious. Or, in technical terms: if we keep feeding our prefrontal cortex consciously, there is no room for the voice of our subconscious. So, "forget about it" does not mean you should abandon your project to go work on something else, or watch TV. It means you should truly give your head some space to do its magic without your active participation. Go for a run, take a shower or meditate.
Whatever works for you.

Keep in mind, those are short term solutions for activating solitude and its benefits. However, most artists agree that you need a ritual of real solitude. This could take the form of writing in a journal every day, taking a stroll, or walking the dog. Any activity that you can commit to daily that releases your head from active duty and from other people's thoughts.

You might find that solitude comes quite naturally to you, or only with incredible difficulty. The opposite of solitude is hard for most people, but just as necessary: confrontation. Whereas solitude releases you from other people's opinions and ideas, as a professional artist and entrepreneur, your work will at some point meet an audience. You will need to get to know this audience and have an idea of what impact your work will have. To get this understanding, you'll need to confront yourself with people, time and time again.

It can be a challenge to find the right harmony between solitude and confrontation. But you will need to. Make room in your routine for specific moments of ultimate peace and quiet. Make room for specific moments to invite feedback and criticism, to question your surroundings and be a critic yourself.

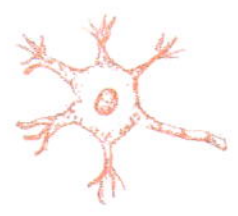

BE
ACTIVE

The importance of being active could be described in basic physics: The more particles there are in a certain environment, the bigger the chance for collision. The more these particles move, the bigger the chance for collision.

Likewise, in your network, the more frequently that people have (recently) heard of you and your work, the bigger the chance that a good opportunity will come along. The more you are active in reaching out to make connections, the bigger the chance for a good opportunity.

Activity leads to opportunities. Remember this very simple rule, and put it into action. Placing your work in your window will add to the number of opportunities. Talking about your work at a party, posting a video on social media, or asking someone a thoughtful question will all work to create opportunities.

HERE ARE A FEW TIPS TO ACTIVATE YOURSELF AND YOUR NETWORK:

• Create a custom postcard with your work on it, and send it to a potential customer.

• Create a (small?) artwork to serve as an introduction of yourself, and send it to someone whose interest you want to catch.

• Ask someone you know to introduce you to a stakeholder you want to connect with.

• Change your profile and cover picture on social media to images that show your artwork, so anyone you connect with will see your work.

• Tweet something about your work, tagging a person you want to meet. That person will receive a notification, so keep it interesting and relevant.

• Make an interesting flyer, like a "REWARD" poster, and hang it in public where your potential customers will see it.

• When you go to an industry event (like a conference, exhibition, etc.), wear a t-shirt with your message on it.

• Create a tribute to one of your stakeholders, combining your message with his/her work. Write a poem or song and publish it.

• Create a blog named after a stakeholder you want to meet, like Xiwanttomeetyou.com, where you blog about all your attempts to meet him/her. Share it.

• Make an announcement on Facebook that you are looking for places to show your work.

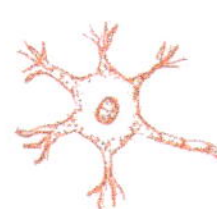

WHERE TO LIVE

Reach out

There are two main reasons for moving somewhere else:

1. To get away from where you are
2. To be somewhere else

Getting away from where you are

We've all heard the story of the 30-year-old who still lives with his/her parents. You might know one first hand – it might even be you! The situation doesn't exactly scream "success". At least, for most of us, it's not how we imagine independence.

Your surroundings have a big influence on your actions. And the environment where you grew up —where you were nurtured, protected and supported—will likely affect your behaviour throughout your life. Imagine moving to a totally different city, like New York or Rome or Beijing, and just how much you would suddenly have to rely on your own abilities. Success would certainly feel like it was of your own making.

A lot of us (especially those from villages) struggle to shake the image we have of ourselves if we stay in the same place. The people we know have come to see us a certain way, and it's all too easy to behave accordingly. A fresh start in a different place can offer the opportunity to create a new perspective of yourself.

Getting to the promised land

The second reason to move is to get closer to what you are looking for. If you live in a small village in Drenthe, Dalarna, Mecklenburg-Vorpommern or Almeria, you might crave a little more action. A bigger city provides more opportunities to meet people, more companies to work for, and easier access to supplies, culture and potential collaborators. On the other hand, if you live in a big city, you might crave more peace and quiet to do your work. As mentioned in the chapter on solitude, it is important to be able to find headspace away from other people and day-to-day distractions, in order to do your work. In short, there is no single 'best' place that works for everyone.

Just remember this: where you live is a choice (unless it's a prison). If you feel a certain place, whether a countryside retreat or an international adventure, might give you the inspiration and opportunities you need… Go for it! No matter what happens, or whether or not it lives up to your expectations, you will take something away from the valuable experience of following your heart.

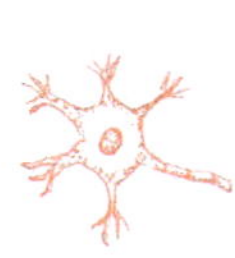

THE PUBLIC VS. ME

"Without deviation from the norm progress is not possible."
—Frank Zappa, Musician, composer, activist and filmmaker, USA

Should I make something the audience likes, or should I make something I like? Artists have always struggled with this question. You can bet that the Egyptians sketching hieroglyphs in the pyramids were already toiling with this dilemma. When there's no food on the table, the answer is easy. When there's a vengeful, vainglorious king who has commissioned his portrait, the answer is easy. But if you're a 21st century artist with tools, freedom and comfort, the answer becomes a lot harder.

Let's start with simply trying to understand your goals; Say you want to be an artist for a living. This means that you need to make work that connects with AN audience. Without an audience, there's no demand, there's no money, there's no work. You are not an artist for a living. You are literally an amateur. To be a professional, your work has to connect with an audience, which of course is not the same thing as producing what they ask you to!

Asking the audience what they want is tricky business. Carmaker Henry Ford supposedly said: "If I had asked people what they wanted, they would have said faster horses." Ford then changed the world not with faster horses, but with his Model T automobile. Similarly, in the '80s, people were polled about the demand for mobile phones. Most people at that time couldn't see the need for having your phone with you all the time.

So where does this leave you? You have to make something for people that they don't know what they want. Yet.

Your job is to find latent needs. Dormant needs. And then to translate those needs into a new language that nobody has ever heard, but understands easily once its spoken.

This makes your intuition your most valuable tool. Soak up your surroundings, absorb the work of others. Experiment and sample the results. Then, let your taste guide you.

Even if a customer comes to you with a clear assignment, you still need to bring those unique qualities that make your work truly yours. And of course, don't forget to keep challenging yourself: If you keep painting the same portrait, even the vain king will get bored. Surprise your customer, exceed their expectations. If can anticipate your customer's needs and solve them before being asked, you might even land your next assignment before you've finished the first.

"I am a firm believer in the philosophy of Kevin Costner's character in the movie Field of Dreams: If you build it, they will come. In other words, it is not just in the making and creating of the work, but the distribution of it. Do you have something to say? Do you care about your subject? Can you communicate relevance? If so, an audience awaits."

Donald Weber,
Photographer and
Educator, Canada

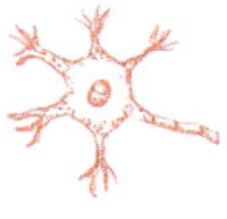

IMPACT AND INFLUENCE

Reach out

Some parts of being an artist give you a clear measurement of success: You make music, people dance… job done. You paint pictures, people stare at them long enough… job done. But if we zoom out a little, there are some bigger matters at stake that are rather harder to measure. How do you see your role as an artist in society? Are you in it to entertain? Are you there to pose questions? Is your role to confront? Or provoke change?

Each of these types of artist has a part to play, but regardless of which one you consider the most important, your personal worldview will give your work its strength. If you believe we should take drastic measures to stop climate change, does that show up in your work? If you feel minorities' rights are a big concern, will you use your art to influence a positive change?

To build your impact and influence, first determine the topics or issues that truly speak to you. Seek out the things that genuinely affect you and are true to your character—your audience will feel your personal commitment, far more than if you are playing with a topic for the sake of being 'socially minded'.

NEXT, DETERMINE WHAT IS YOUR ROLE AS AN ARTIST:

• I just want to create my work and get it out there

• I want people to be touched by my work

• I want commercial success

• I want acknowledgement and to create new opportunities for myself

• I want to make change beyond my work

Then, find like-minded people to help build and amplify your message. Look beyond your discipline to collaborate on a common or shared goal, based on how you see your role. Then, work together to create artwork that will engage an audience.

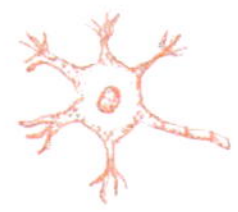

THE
WORLD

THE WORLD

So far, the focus has been on you and what personal skills, attitudes and knowledge you can work on to become a stronger creative entrepreneur. Ready or not, now we'll step out into **THE WORLD**. Maybe you're already out there, or perhaps you're still in the safety of the cocoon called art school, but in either case, let's now look at the external factors to face.

The world is where your art finds its relevance and your goals are realised. It is here that you find your collaboration partners and other stakeholders. (Yes, your friends live in the world too; they're your social capital.) The world is where you share and promote your work, it's where you find your venues and audiences, and it's where your clients live and where money exists. It's here that you pay your bills, taxes and bookkeeper, and also where to find a support network and institutions that can help. It is here that you negotiate contracts, protect your copyrights and make sure you get paid.

But, don't worry: you don't have to know it all when you step into the world. You will learn by doing. Just make sure you know enough to realise when to ask for help and when there's still something you need to learn.

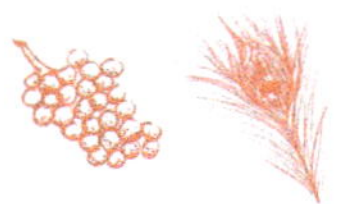  

STAKE HOLDERS

Stakeholders are all the people who have an interest or concern (a stake) in your work or your career. The obvious ones are (potential) clients and the decision-makers at venues, galleries, agencies and any other places key to your success. If you think more widely about all of those who can impact your career, it also includes collaborators, rivals, and city officials. Start to consider your current social capital, the people you have already surrounded yourself with. Then, see how to expand your network, so you can find the right people to learn from, collaborate with, and sell your work to.

SOCIAL CAPITAL

Stakeholders

When looking for a job, the more social capital you have, the better your chance of success. This means having a network that's not only wide, but deep: friends, family members, and neighbours that you're closely connected to. These are the people who know your wants and needs, and are willing to help. Social capital is about the number of connections you have and the strength of those connections.

It's not just about being the life of the party, it's about building relationships. If you're the positive, talkative type and you come from a family of successful entrepreneurs or artists, chances are that building social capital comes as second nature to you, and your existing social capital is already quite an asset. If you're more of an introvert, or if you're surrounded by people who constantly struggle to achieve, or would rather complain about the way things are than fixing them, you will need to work a little harder to gain some social capital. Seek out wealth in all its forms—ideas, positivity, resources, knowledge, experience, etc.—and cultivate your own wealth too, so you have something to give back. The people in your life are resources you can draw from, and vice versa, so make it a part of your practice to build and nurture connections.

What are some ways to reinforce the positive relationships you have?
How can you expand your network with new people?

In a class of 60 students, I demonstrated the power of social capital by making a bold request: I asked for a sailing boat and a shipping container. I couldn't easily access either item by myself, but when I put the request to a group of 60 people, I was able to get a shipping container and had my choice between two
sailing boats.

The more people you know, who know what you need and want to help you, the better your chance of successfully getting it.

"The support network that you have is much more important than you realise. You can help each other in a very practical way."

**Melissa Henderson,
Visual Artist, Sweden**

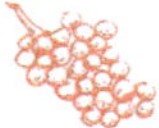

COL LABOR ATION

Stakeholders

There are many forms of collaboration. Beyond working with others in your own discipline, there's also collaborations that are cross-, multi-, inter- and transdisciplinary, and so on. The options are numerous and sometimes vague (yet worth looking up), but the underlying motivation is the same: together we are stronger. Working together, your ideas and abilities are amplified. You have more to say, more ways of saying it and more people that you can reach. Working with others also means having to negotiate between yourselves and share any earnings afterward, so before you set off together, be sure you set clear expectations and terms for smooth sailing.

Diversify

Find people that do not think and work exactly like you do. It may be pleasing to see our interests and attitudes reflected back in others, but it will not push you toward the best result. People who know things you don't know, people who like things you don't like, and people who have different skillsets than yours are more likely to supplement you as an artist and an entrepreneur. You can inspire true creativity in each other, as you each work from your own perspective. Whether working with a specialist in another field, a practitioner in another discipline, or someone from another culture, you can give to each other a new and unique perspective on problem-solving, creation and your work.

Architect David Adjaye and his composer brother Peter worked together on an album where they explore the relationship between sound and space. PJ Harvey and photographer Seamus Murphy teamed up for their project The Hollow of the Hand, combining poetry and pictures. If you are the expert within your field, you can deepen your work through collaboration with other art disciplines. Or take it a step further and work with a scientist, psychologist or philosopher.

Unify

Artists often benefit from coming together for like-minded goals, for example finding a place to work, raising visibility, or getting feedback. Think about what your own needs are, and realise there are more than likely a lot of other artists who are in search of that very same thing. Get the ball rolling: start a collective, organise a workshop or feedback sessions, create a festival or an exhibition to get work seen. If you're looking for a working space, find other people with similar or complementary skills and help each other. This not only helps with your goal of finding a working space, but also builds a community in which every visitor is a double opportunity, as well. A lot of success is bred by coming together, creating hotspots of creativity: Portishead and Tricky set up the trip hop scene in Bristol; The Hacienda nightclub of Manchester (check out the movie "24 Hour Party People"); The Dusseldorf School of Photography studied at the same art academy in the mid-1970s.

WHO TO WORK WITH

Stakeholders

Nobody becomes successful entirely on their own. From birth to death, other people bring to you support that you may not have even realised you were missing, whether it's technical, practical, emotional, etc. So, to give your projects a better chance of success, make it a priority to always be meeting people. You never know when they'll be able to help you along, and hopefully you can help them, too. While the last chapter on Collaboration is about teaming up with someone so that together you can amplify your message, this chapter is about making strategic choices on who you surround yourself with.

Who you need to work with

It is essential to have a clear grasp on who runs the business you are in. When you start out in music, for example, you might think that the only person who's important is the record label boss, but once you dive in, you meet A&R managers, sync-deal agents, publishers, front of house managers, festival programmers and an array of other people who can profoundly influence your success. It is no different in the art world, in commercial photography, or in any other industry. So, do your homework: speak to others who are starting out, read biographies of those in the business, volunteer at a venue. Ask and ask and ask. Build up a map of the people who can influence your career.

Who you want to work with

Now try thinking from a different angle. Ask yourself, "If I could work with anyone in the world, who would that be?" It doesn't necessarily have to be someone in your same discipline—remember, you can work across boundaries—but it may help if you start with your passion. Who truly inspires you? If your answer is Bob Marley, or some other artist who's already deceased, then take note about why you would've loved to work with him, and what you would've gained from it. Can you find someone else who could give you something similar?

• What can I do on my own?

• What do I need other people for?

• Who are the people that can help me?

• What do I want from those people and what do I have to offer in return?

• How can I get on their radar?

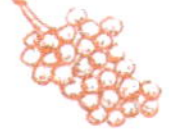

HIRE THE HELP

"Find people you trust. You cannot be good at everything."

Reinout Douma, Composer & Conductor, The Netherlands

You should understand the basics of your craft, your rights, your money and your time, but you don't have to be a master at every single aspect of your work and your industry. You can outsource tasks you don't want to do, or aren't very good at, to experts and specialists, freeing yourself to focus on what you do best.

Accountant
An accountant can help with your bookkeeping and money management. They can also support with financial decisions like buying or renting a house, renovating a studio or opening a shop.

Manager
A good manager will help get your business organised and running smoothly. Hiring one will cost you some income, but if they're good at their job, will eventually make you money. Not to mention save you some stress.

Agent
An agent is out in the field trying to get you work. A good agent is well connected and can get you opportunities easily that would be hard to get on your own. Agents usually take a percentage of your income. Make sure the agent has an incentive to work specifically for you.

Publisher
A publisher is someone who takes your creative output (be it photos, music or a book) and makes it into saleable products. A publisher puts in serious work and money (some will pay a band/writer/artist an advance) and so will want a serious cut of the income as well.

Assistant
Having someone keep track of what you're up to and what you need to do can vastly improve your productivity. An assistant role could also be done by an intern.

Communication and P.R. expert
This person has the role of getting word about you into the world. Someone that can manage your social media profile, get you interviews and come up with ideas to get you and your work noticed.

Mentor
A mentor is someone further down the road than you who wants to help you grow as an artist. It's a relationship usually based on trust and goodwill, rather than payment, with someone you click well with. Ask nicely, and you may be surprised how much people enjoy helping.

Grant expert
There are people and companies that help you find grants or subsidies for your work. If they do good work, this service can pay for itself.

THE AUDIENCE(S)

Stakeholders

Many artists get so preoccupied with making their work that they forget to think about who they're making it for. While entrepreneurs take for granted that they need to define a target audience or target groups for their products, this is something often overlooked in the creative industry. But, when you put something into the world, you need to have an idea of who your audience is.

Creating for an audience

You can produce work first, and then seek out the audience best suited for it when you're ready to share, or, you can look at the demands of a specific audience and produce work based on that. This doesn't fit everyone's creative process, but some may find it inspiring,
as well as a clear-cut way of speaking directly to an audience.

Reaching out to your audience

Thinking that your art is interesting for everyone is, quite simply, a mistake. The better you can understand who your audience is, and target them, the better engagement you will get.

Once you know who your audience is, it will help you know how and where to reach them. For example, the best place to reach your audience may be in a museum, a bar, in a children's bookstore, on chocolate packaging, or on the street. Make a conscious choice based on the best way to experience your work and who you think it can reach.

Sharp shooting

A target audience of "culturally interested 20 to 40 year olds" is way too broad. Narrow it down – what is your real goal? One example of micro-targeting is a billboard printed with the name of the president of a big company, placed along his usual commute to work. If the attention of this one person is worth so much, spend it on a campaign that is sure to reach him.

Find innovative ways to pinpoint your target audience. Find Facebook groups or forums based on a specific topic, for example. Or find events where the chance of interest in your work is significantly higher than elsewhere.

One way to better target your audience is to focus on interest intersections. For example, if you're a photographer who takes pictures of landscapes that you digitally alter into fantasy worlds, you've got three keywords for specific target audiences: photography, digital manipulation and fantasy. Try to find groups online that are interested in at least two of these three topics, and you've got a well-defined target audience, already much better than a generic 'museum visitor'.

When putting your work out to the world, always ask yourself: am I shooting with buckshot or do I have specific targets?

PROMO TION

To get noticed, above and beyond the many that crave attention, is a very challenging task. While big companies have a budget to hire ad agencies, PR firms and marketing advisors to get the word out about their products, you probably won't be able to start out with that luxury. But, not to worry: in the digital age the world is at your fingertips. It starts with embracing the idea of you as a brand. That includes how you present yourself on- and off-line. Start by re-thinking what you share on social media and becoming more conscious about your web presence. Getting yourself and your work in the public eye is a great challenge but a priceless investment. Nowadays, as companies battle it out for people's attention, we see it's quite possibly the most expensive asset in the world.

A CONSISTENT BRAND

Promotion

"It's not what you are that counts, it's what they think you are."
—Andy Warhol

Whenever you see someone for the first time, whether you want to or not, you instantly categorise them, whether as a potential threat, a potential lover or anything in between. You assess certain clues, like how the person walks and moves, how they're dressed, their facial expression, what actions they're taking, where they are, or even how other people are reacting.

The same goes whenever we encounter something new. Take for example an experiment that was done with the famous violin player Joshua Bell. He played in the subway. Even though on that same day he had a sold out performance in a grand theatre, in the subway very few people stopped and listened to him. Outside of the right context, in a refined theatre surrounded by an attentive audience, he wasn't recognised or appreciated in nearly the same way.

The impression you make is based on you, the product you make AND how it's presented.

The impression people get is based on concepts and associations they already have, like: someone wearing a tie is business-like, something presented on a silk pillow is valuable, someone playing in the subway is not good enough for a theatre.

A brand is an idea that floats somewhere between you and the person observing you, and is based both on the signals you send and the ideas that the receiver has in her or his head. You can control most of the signals that you send, so the more you work to ensure they're consistent, the better the odds that what you want to communicate is what is actually being received.

Keep in mind, too, that your brand should be not only consistent and strong, but also noticeable and unique. For example, as a man, wearing a suit might easily create for you a brand as a 'businessman', but not necessarily one of distinction. You will be identified easily, but remembered poorly.

"Branding is not about marketing. In the arts, it's about personality."

**Reinout Douma,
Composer and
Conductor,
The Netherlands**

"Everybody is a brand. The way you dress and the way you are is your brand."

**Javier Medina,
Founder of Amodal Company, Spain**

BE VISIBLE

If you're invisible, nobody can see you. That seems like stating the obvious, right? Yet, lots of people expect to be seen even while flying under the radar.

Say you're looking for someone who plays guitar. The first person who pops into your head will be either very close to you, or very active on social media. Off the top of your head, you can probably come up with a few more names. If you were to take your address book and actively search for someone who plays the guitar, or even call everyone you know, you'd find a lot more guitarists. There are a lot of guitarists out there, if you go hunting for them.

Yet, you probably wouldn't go to all that trouble – you might very well stop thinking about it after the first couple of names that came into your head easily. The people who you think of within 30 seconds are called "top of mind", in marketing lingo. The people who you thought of later hardly matter. The people you had to actively scout for don't matter at all.

How many people know what you do? How many of them would have you top of mind? Is it enough to sustain a business? You might be more invisible than you think. Fortunately, there are numerous ways to make yourself more visible.

Exhibit your work

When you first start out, show your work whenever you get the chance, even in small venues or unusual places like libraries or cafes. The more eyes (or ears) on your work, the better.

Publish

Get your name out there. For example, write an article about your work, your experiences or your philosophies. Be sure it offers something valuable to the public (self-promotion rarely does). Websites that publish you will often credit your name and website. Even better, if you have some big news, write a press release and target relevant media, so they'll write about you or your work as proper journalism or art criticism.

Blog

A variant on publishing: start a blog or vlog. The upside is that you decide what and when you publish about yourself and your work. The downside is that you have to find your own audience.

Contests

In most creative fields, there are numerous contests. The impact of winning depends on how well the contest publicises itself and who is in the jury, so pay attention to the stakes before entering. Fair warning, many contests charge a submission fee; if so, consider if it's really worth entering.

Network

Nothing gets you on people's radar like meeting them face-to-face, so invest some time and money in attending festivals, openings and social gatherings. Hanging out with your customers, peers and competitors in an informal way will help them to remember you and your work.

Present yourself

All these actions rely in one way or another on you presenting yourself and your work well. So get honest feedback from people who know how to present well and make sure your story comes off as it should. Alternatively, go Daft Punk: hide your face, decline interviews, be an enigma.

Website / Social Media

If you want people to Google you or contact you, an active online presence is necessary.

YOUR WEB PRESENCE

Before you start actively reaching out to other people, you need to have a baseline presence. If someone does a search for you online, your first hit shouldn't be a YouTube video uploaded six years ago of you goofing around at a campsite, it should be your own website and supporting professional profiles (LinkedIn, Soundcloud, YouTube, Vimeo, etc).

Register a domain name for your website that is preferably: short, pronounceable, hard to missspell and is based on your name or your work.

HERE'S A FEW TIPS ON BUILDING YOUR WEB PRESENCE:

01. The work is most important
People visit your website for practical reasons; they want to see the work you have made, so put that front and centre. Make sure that the images or video you use are of high quality. Give people the information they need: How big is this in real life? Did you make it for a client? Is it for sale? What is the title? When did you make it?

02. You matter too
The maker of the product always adds to (or subtracts from) the value. So, tell your audience who you are, what you have done and why your work is valuable. If possible, do this in ways that offer an objective viewpoint rather than tooting your own horn. For example, include a recommendation by a client, a review by a critic, etc. If you have achievements like awards, impressive clients or exhibitions under your belt, include them. There are many tips online for how to write an artist's statement and CV; do some research and adapt what works for you.

03. Quality vs quantity
Make a good edit of your work: try to show the range of your professional work, but keep it sharp and focused. If you struggle to produce a good edit, consider working with a professional editor. You want your viewers to think that you know what 'good' means and to be left wanting more. If you produce very different kinds of work (say, 'product photography' and 'spoken words poetry') you may consider setting up two websites to keep it focused.

04. Call to action
If people are impressed by what they have seen, they need an easy way to act upon it. At the very least you should give them the option to call and email you. But ideally it's even easier: set up a webshop that lets them buy something directly from the site, or a calendar that lets them make an appointment. Make it easy for your visitor to become your client.

SOCIAL MEDIA

There are online public platforms for every type of artist: currently, for example, musicians are on Bandcamp and Soundcloud, filmmakers are on YouTube and Vimeo. So, part of the work of knowing what's going on in your industry is to keep on top of the platforms, both making your own profile and learning from the people who use the platform well.

Nowadays, it's pretty easy to upload your movie to YouTube and Vimeo, to give it a nice title, descriptions and keywords and then post them on Twitter and Facebook. So, congratulations, you've mastered the basics of social media… but welcome to the club. So has everyone else. If this is your only strategy, your chances of standing out from the crowd are slim.

THERE ARE A LOT OF BOOKS AND WEBSITES (BOTH GREAT AND AWFUL) ON GETTING THE BEST OUT OF SOCIAL MEDIA. DO YOUR RESEARCH, BUT HERE'S A FEW TIPS TO GET STARTED.

01. Content strategy and calendar
If you use a social media platform, make sure you really do use it. Nothing screams "I don't care" like a YouTube channel that was last updated two years ago. When you decide to start using any given social media, make a plan. What's your content strategy for the platform? When will you post what kind of material? Steal from the best, and rework it to something that suits you and your workflow. Make a calendar of your future posts.

02. Targeting and timing
When you post, take into account who will be ideally seeing your updates, and when. If there are certain key dates or events in your industry, get to know them and post accordingly. Are you
attracting the attention of possible new clients (at the beginning of their journey)? Are you including your recent clients (at the beginning of a working relationship)? Are you improving your brand by showing how successful you are in turning one-time clients into repeat customers?

03. Tone of voice and content choice
Make sure that what typifies your work, also typifies your social media posts. For example if all your songs are about love, make sure your posts reflect the same sensitivity. If you like to paint desolate industrial buildings, don't be all happy-go-lucky on Facebook. Your social media use should make it easier to understand your work. Also, keep in mind that you don't have to make all your posts original content, you can also share things that are relevant.

04. Transfer from social media to real life
Your social media presence can be a gateway that encourages people to get to know you off-screen. Mention places you are going to be. If you organise events online, interact with people who are also going to come. Look for opportunities to transfer online interaction to real life interaction.

Promotion

TIMING

The key to generating buzz is timing: it's better to have 100 people talking about you in one day than 200 people over the span of a year. This is why execs from every creative industry, whether it's Hollywood or Apple, try to control leaks about their new releases. Likewise, you might try to manage your promotion so it gives you peaks of interest, rather than ongoing mild interest. It might sound counterintuitive, but sometimes it's a better plan to build up some quiet and calm, and then make a big splash with your announcement using all your social media, press releases, video, etc.

Apart from the rhythm of your communication, the date, day and time of your promotion also make a difference. There is plenty of research on the timing of social media posts, for example, showing that depending on your target demographic, you'll get better results on certain days and at certain times. Students might be open to your message at 10 in the morning, while most working people are not.

But, don't just look at the statistics. Try to understand your particular audience. Are they night creatures? Do they want something they can share, or something that feels like a message just between you and them? Is there a conversation going, or are you just broadcasting things at them at random intervals?

Try to find the sweet spot, too, between posting too often and not enough. Creating a comfortable frequency will help your audience to feel engaged without being smothered or spammed. Timing influences the appreciation of a relationship, so be sensitive to the impact of your promotion on your audience and take feedback very seriously.

FAN  OWN ERSHIP

One way to transform your 'audience' into your 'fans' is to give them a sense of ownership. Nowadays, people are inundated constantly with messages from products and services, making it easier to get lost in the noise. When your fans have a sense of ownership in what's happening—because they've met you or seen you in person, because you talk with them in social media or asked for their opinion—it is easier to keep interacting because they're invested in the outcome. You don't have to shout if you are already talking to someone.

The idea of having a running conversation with people is what drives a lot of strategic thinking on social media. Try to think of ways to be personal in the interactions you have with your audience, and invite their thoughts or involvement. Let's say you're designing a new album cover. Why not ask your audience for tips on designers, or even hold a contest among your fans to design the work themselves? Either way, you've got them feeling like they're a part of your creative process. The loyalty they feel as co-owners will mean that they won't only buy your album, they'll also promote the album to their friends and networks for you! Meet and greets, personal messages, merchandise, these are all opportunities to invite people to feel ownership of what you do.

MO NEY

Unless you fake your death, live off-grid and become self-sustainable, money is, for better or worse, a daily reality of modern society. Even if you don't want it to influence your life, it is a factor that needs to be taken into account. There are a few basics you need to understand and work with, like how much money is needed to support your lifestyle. For many financial matters, it's also possible (and sometimes advisable) to hire an expert. Your creativity will definitely come in handy when it comes to finding new avenues of making money.

KEEP IT Money BASIC

In an interview with the magazine Intersection, actor Giovanni Ribisi tells the story of his wake-up call regarding money. He has been an actor since he was a child, so there had always been someone to look at his contracts, invest his money, and do his financial homework. However, a turning point came when Giovanni was working on the set of Gone In 60 Seconds, in which he needed to learn to strip and rebuild a car. It was then that he realised he'd been driving cars for a long time without knowing even the basics about how they worked. The same went for most of his financial dealings. He had no idea how much money he made, how much he needed and where it went. He decided to take control of his finances by learning about the moving parts, understanding the consequences of his decisions, and then choosing for himself what was best.

Likewise, to have control over your own financial life, you need to know the basics. That doesn't mean necessarily that you have to manage your financial life yourself, but you do need to know enough to make the right decisions. That means being able to understand the moving parts that influence the outcome, or being able to ask questions until you do understand enough. So, for example, if you're talking with a financial advisor for your business or when buying a house, don't let yourself be intimidated or embarrassed if she starts speaking in a language you don't understand—ask to clarify. Understand enough about how the car runs so you can still be in control. If you find yourself in a complex situation with money being spent and allocated in a way you don't understand, or any other deal that feels even remotely shady, stop and bring in an expert who is motivated to be on your side, who can explain things and advocate for your priorities.

Money shouldn't rule your life.
You should rule your money.

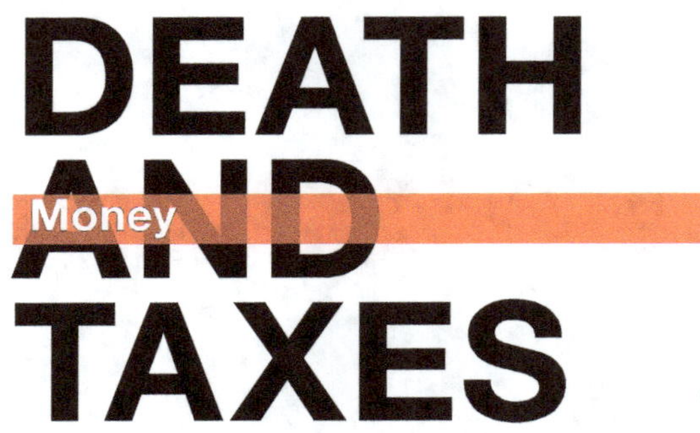

DEATH AND TAXES

Money

"In this world nothing can be said to be certain, except death and taxes."
—Benjamin Franklin

THERE ARE A FEW BASIC THINGS YOU SHOULD KNOW ABOUT MONEY:

• When you make money, the state will want a percentage of it as income tax.

• When you spend money for your business, you may be able to declare it as a business expense, which reduces your taxes.

There is much more you can learn about how to do your bookkeeping, but the question is if it's worth learning everything yourself. Many will tell you that a good accountant pays for herself, because there are many ins and outs you have to know when filing your taxes, and checking the right boxes will save you money. You can take a course and spend hours learning it yourself, or you can pay someone else to be the expert for you. When starting out you will probably pay your accountant a few hundred euros a year. It might feel like a lot, but if you count on this annual expense and make sure to put money aside, it will save you a lot of hours and headache. But here's a crash course in the basics:

Taxes
Taxes are inevitable, so the best way to handle your income tax is to figure out what bracket of income tax you're in, and then, each time a payment comes in, set that percentage aside in a separate account. A good guideline is to save 1/3 of your income for taxes. This way, you'll have the amount due ready to pay, with as few unpleasant surprises as possible. If you have a more complicated situation, hire an accountant to help. Also learn the difference between VAT and income tax; as a small business owner or freelancer you will have to deal with both.

Invoices and receipts
Keep all your invoices and receipts. It's legally required to keep them (for at least five years in the Netherlands). There are apps available to help with your administration, including archival for receipts and writing and sending your invoices, that can save you many precious hours.

MO' MONEY, LESS HOURS

Money

To know how much money you need to make to support your lifestyle, you need to know how much your lifestyle costs.

It comes down to this: You go broke when you spend more money than you have. The key to not going broke is to earn more money than you spend. It's one of those seemingly obvious ideas, that's nevertheless hard to put into practice. Laid out here is a simple exercise we will help you get a grip on the amount of money you need to make to support your lifestyle.

Over the course of a month, keep track of all the money you spend (if you pay for everything by card this is a pretty straightforward exercise) on essentials, like food, insurance, rent, gas / electricity, and transportation. Now, take the total of your essential expenses and add 20% as a buffer. This will give you a very rough estimate of how much money you need to make every month to avoid going broke. Be sure to factor in your income tax.

Suppose you need 1250 euros a month minimum to support the essentials of your lifestyle. Adding a buffer of 20% to this would give you 1500 euros. If you've got an income tax rate of let's say 25%, that means you need an income of 2000 euros per month to give you some stability.

Working by the hour
If you work by the hour, you can make an easy calculation of what your minimum hourly rate should be to earn this minimum income. Give yourself a buffer of 40% when it comes to time, because you'll need time for administration, sales and marketing, writing proposals, and other non-billable chores.

So, let's say you can reasonably expect 24 billable hours a week. That means, to make ends meet, you need to set your minimum wage at 21 euros per hour. That is, 2000 euros / (24 hours X 4 weeks in a month) = 21.00 euro.

Working by gigs or sales
If you play gigs or sell works, make a plausible estimate of the number of gigs/works you can sell each month. For example, suppose you can play 4 gigs a month as a solo artist, this means you need to get 400 - 500 euros per gig.

Keep in mind, these calculations don't give you any weeks off for holidays or illness. To give yourself time off, or a wider buffer for other activities or expenses (like a house or a kid), you'll want to increase how much you earn per hour/gig.

ALTERNATIVE PAYMENT

Money

"Cash rules everything around me, C.R.E.A.M. Get the money, dollar dollar bill, y'all"
—Wu-Tang Clan

Money is an imaginary concept – it doesn't really have any value, except we all agree that it does, so it works as a tool of exchange. The basic idea is: you have something that somebody else wants, she gives you money for it. There are variations, however. You can rent things, for example. You can barter, or work for 'exposure' or a 'favour'. Payment isn't just one thing.

Pay what you want

One way of pricing your products and services is 'pay what you want', which lets your customer set the price. Most people are afraid that if they don't set the price themselves, they'll be
underpaid, but artists who sell their merchandise after shows often make more money this way. The amount that people pay is often directly related to their admiration for you as an artist, rather than the work's economic value.

Rent out

Instead of selling someone your work, you could also rent it. Or, another option is rent-to-own, whereby if they've rented it long enough, they've essentially bought it.

Scarcity

Scarcity adds to the value of work, so use it to your advantage. Sign and edition your work, or release special editions. In one famous example, the Wu-Tang Clan released an album of which there was only one copy, 'The Wu – Once Upon A Time In Shaolin', which sold for $2 million.

Circumvent overhead

Look for opportunities where you can cut out the middleman. Platforms and agents often take a hefty cut – see what you can do to reduce, if not eliminate, the overhead fees and reach your audience directly.

Work for free

If you would like to work for a certain client or would like to see your work in a certain museum or on a specific stage, why not give them a free sample? Think of it as an investment in a longer-term relationship. Offer a client a free month of work as an opportunity to prove yourself, donate a work to the museum, or give a free concert on the street outside the venue you want to play.

Crowdfunding

One way that you can ensure demand for your project is crowdfunding. This will let you pre-sell your products before you pay to produce them, so you already have a good idea what your return on investment will be. There are a lot of online crowdfunding platforms (for example, Indiegogo and Kickstarter) that make this as painless as possible, but you could also try to find investors yourself.

Sponsors

A sponsor pays you in exchange for promoting their product or cause. This usually involves a mention of their brand name along with your publications, but you'll want to make sure the terms of their sponsorship are clear to you. Some newer formats involve more of a collaborative effort.

Grants

A grant is basically sponsorship by the government or an organisation that wants to support you or your project. Some grants are no-strings-attached, but others have conditions. Be sure you understand what your obligations are.

No concessions

There is also the option of self-financing, which is to say you work a day job to pay for your creative work and are therefore able to keep your art and income separate. This gives you the freedom to make what you want without making concessions to a client or customer, but obviously you need another source of income, which will absorb some of your time.

Expert View:

"Sponsors? Sure, why not!? But only if they don't have requirements on how my work should look. If I have to tattoo a Sony logo on my ass, then maybe not. You have to constantly make moral judgments."
Jonas Liveröd, Artist working with sculpture, drawing and installation, Sweden

SEC URITY

So, you know what you want and you are going for it. Great! Let's just take a moment to do some risk management. It may sound like boring bureaucracy, but should the day come that a client changes their mind, you'll be grateful when you have a good contract to fall back on. You'll be relieved to know how to protect your copyrights when someone tries to steal your ideas, and have peace of mind with insurance when you break that expensive vase on assignment, or break a leg and can't go to work. And, Future You will thank you when you've got enough in the bank to retire. Being an entrepreneur involves taking risks, but don't be foolish. Take smart, calculated risks to know the reward will be worth it.

"Starting an art biz while still working a day job is absolutely possible. You'll need a few things: a vision for what you're working toward, passion as fuel, and commitment to go the distance one small step at a time."
—Kelly Rae Roberts, Artist and Social Worker, USA

Choosing to be an artist does not necessarily mean taking a decision that rules out other possibilities. There are lots of artists who, alongside their personal practice, also teach, work in production or do commercial jobs. There are examples of artists with long careers in totally unrelated fields before turning to art, like Paul Gauguin, who was a stockbroker for more than a decade before he became a painter. There are still other artists who start a business on the side, like Damien Hirst, the artist and restaurateur, or Raphael Lyon, who grows sculptures using geologic processes, and as a side business ferments honey and herbs into wine.

Any art teacher you encounter was also likely trained to be an artist. When they encourage you to pursue your dreams without compromise, keep in mind that it's a message they're also repeating to themselves. Their choice to teach reflects the evolving needs of an artist over a lifetime of making work and paying bills; rather than thinking of that as a compromise, it may help you to consider what it gives to an artist to be able to help others along their path. Supporting roles such as teaching, editing, producing, publishing, etc., often enrich one's own practice.

A mixed practice can consist of two very different things, or two roles closely linked. You can combine your work as an artist with a desk job, or there are also examples of artists joining forces to run a shop with their own products, allowing them to keep up their art production while sharing the shop responsibilities.

In the first few pages of this book, we talked about the idea of success. This will involve an ongoing search for balance: between risk and security, between creative freedom and money in the bank, between time spent on your work and time with your family. Ultimately, the only one who can decide the right balance for you, is you.

WHO HAS YOUR BACK?

Security

In a regular 9-to-5 job, there are a few upsides and a lot of them have to do with security. When you get sick, for example, you call your boss, go back to bed and still get paid. If you make a stupid mistake on a project and lose a client, you're not the one who's legally responsible, your company is. You get paid time off, and in some cases a summer allowance or a yearly bonus. When you retire, you'll most likely get a pension.

If you're self-employed, on the other hand, you likely get none of the above.

Saving for a rainy day

So, there are a few things that you need to do in order to create your own security. For example, because your income is a variable, the money you earn each month should be significantly higher than that of a steady job. Your savings account should be a bit fatter than most, too.

No matter how you organise your money, you don't have to assume that it's all doom and gloom. Talk with your friends and family, too, and ensure you've got safety nets. Have a plan that you could put into motion if you were to fall ill next month.

Insurance

Even though you're liable for your own disability, long-term sickness and legal issues, a lot of freelancers do not insure themselves, and that's a huge risk to take. There are some alternatives, like Bread Funds, which is a lot like an insurance, but on a smaller scale and with like-minded people.

Insurance against legal costs is a lot cheaper. Whether you need it or not depends on the type of projects you take: with smaller and independent projects you can afford to have a misstep, whereas with large corporations, there's less room for error. It may not be a fun thing to have a conversation about, but talk this through with an expert.

Pension and retirement

If you are past 30 years old: think of how you can retire. Is there a point at which you can just sit back and reminisce about your creative journey when you are older and wiser? Work towards funding this.

Liability and contracts

There are also institutions that have your back when it comes to copyright, for example, or for drafting contracts. In most countries there are unions and organisations that support artists with copyright management, such as Pictoright, DuPho and BNO in the Netherlands, ADAGP in France, SABAM and SOFAM in Belgium, DACS in the UK, Bild-Kunst in Germany and many more. These organisations are usually membership-based, however, and/or may require that the artist give them (exclusive) rights to manage primary rights. They also usually offer legal advice and try to achieve better copyright protection for artists by lobbying and pushing for legislation.

"As a freelancer it's important to have backup strategies in case something happens to you. I have insurance, so if I fall ill I would get an income. You need to take care of it, because we never know what may happen tomorrow."

Anna-Maria Helsing, Conductor, Finland

RISK/ REWARD

A lot of the stories you hear about artists who make it are high stakes fairy tales: An actress who leaves everything and everyone behind to move to Hollywood and is then discovered; an artist who puts the last of his money into his project and then finally becomes a hit. They make for great stories, mostly because they skip the boring bits and have a happy ending. The truth is, when you start asking successful artists how they got to where they are, there's far more stories involving 'good luck' and 'hard work' as central characters. Some were blessed by being born into artist families with good connections, some slaved away for years before getting any kind of recognition, and many faced rejection again and again before being 'discovered'.

Here's another romantic success story: Musician Henry Rollins (Black Flag) used to scoop ice cream before he decided in 1981 that a life in music was worth the risk of skipping a day of work at Häägen-Dazs: "I looked at the ice cream scoop in my hand…my chocolate-bespattered apron…and my future in the world of minimum wage work…or I could go up to New York and audition for this crazy band who was my favorite. What's the worst that's gonna happen to me? I miss a day of work…ooh, there goes 21 bucks."

Put in those terms, it seems like an easy choice to make: a low risk, potential big reward. Perhaps it seems even clearer to us now, because we know he ended up succeeding. Maybe some other people skipped work that day, and didn't get the job.

We're constantly tasked with evaluating risk and reward, and trying to make the right choice. Missing out on one day of work doesn't seem so bad, but for others, the risk is literally life and death. Journalists, for example, can be placed in life-threatening situations for their work, and must also ask themselves when the reward is worth the risk. Photojournalist Lynsey Addario said that it's hard to explain why it's worth the risk, except to say it's a cause she believes in. "There are so many people who go through life and never find a calling but anyone who is driven by something larger than themselves will understand."

There is no one piece of advice to give when it comes to the balance between risk and reward. You can play by the rules and make it. Or fail. You can gamble your life savings and win, or lose. There are no guarantees, there are no sure-fire strategies.

When there's something you really want to achieve…
Consider what you stand to lose if you go for it.
Consider what you stand to gain if you go for it.
And make a decision.

Security
CON
TRACTS

When you make something, you're entitled to certain legal rights. In some industries, like music, the rules are more complicated because there are rights for composing the song, for performing it and for recording it for the first time. In some industries like visual arts, when you make a photo or a painting, you just have copyright. Each of these rights, and their worth, are stated and negotiated in contracts.

Maud van der Leeuw, a legal expert specialised in intellectual property law for artists, says that (starting) artists often fail to make clear agreements, when it comes to protecting their copyrights. This means that you might only find out later, when things have gone wrong, that you've given away far more than you planned. Another common mistake is not realising that copyright covers the form or manner in which an idea is expressed, not the idea itself. When pitching an idea to a potential client, it's important to keep this in mind and to be careful about what you say and don't say, or they may take the idea without actually hiring you.

In all partnerships, rights management and contracts are a part of doing business, so you'll need to know what you're getting yourself into. For example, if you're a musician, a label that wants to produce your music will also want a share of the profits for sales, broadcast and streaming. For all rights, you need to agree on the amount of money involved.

Or, if you're a visual artist, and someone wants to use your photo or design in a book, magazine or on a website, they need to ask your permission. You then need to negotiate costs and usage for your work to protect it. For example, is it a one-time usage, or an ongoing license? How many copies will they make and distribute? Can they use your image on the cover, or in advertisements? To make sure that the contract suits you and is fair, you will definitely want to get help from a specialist focused on creative industries.

The basics of a contract are very simple: you give something away and you get something in return. Always make sure you understand completely what you are giving away and what you are getting in return. Are you licensing your work for use (which is like hiring) or transferring the rights (which is like selling)? Different rights have different values, so make sure you're getting fair compensation.

In signing a contract, the most important thing is that you feel comfortable with the people you're in partnership with. Anyone you sign a contract with is someone who could potentially be your adversary in court, so listen to your gut. This is just as important as the fine print.

Make sure you understand the incentives for the person on the other side of the table. Will she make money even if she doesn't do anything to help you? Does he have motivation to maximise your success? For example, the prime objective of an agent may be to represent as many creatives as possible, to offer clients a wide selection. This arrangement leaves little motivation to help you specifically, and works mainly to benefit him and his clients, at the expense of your work.

getting out the greenhouse
creative capital
f
in
Etsy
challenge
EXPERT

AFTER WORD

Whether you flipped through the pages, read every single page, or tasted only the bits that seemed appetising to you, the real work starts now.

Knowledge and ideas are only meaningful when they are brought into action. So do yourself a favour and flip back, and make note of what you found the most annoying. Usually, where there is friction, there is work to be done. Then, mark the things that most piqued your interest.

For each of the parts you have marked, both annoying and inspiring, write down the questions you have. For example:
"Who do I know that has intricate knowledge of the art market?"
"Is there a bread fund I could participate in?"
"Do my clients perceive me as a true professional?"

Don't worry about answering them right now. Just write down all the questions that can help. Your next task will be to find a friend, a colleague, or a family member with whom you can discuss how to get some answers.

Also, take some time to go back to the prologue and reconsider your idea of success. Give yourself the option to already revise what you want, and complete these sentences:

My idea of success is ____________________________

To get there I need to __________________________

The first step I can take is _______________________

A skill I already possess (that will work in my favour) is ________________

Set clear goals, make them achievable and fun. Dare to dream big and envision the road to get there. Revisit this every year.

NOW GET OUT THERE, THE WORLD AWAITS!
P.S. If you haven't discovered our activity cards yet, do so at el-art.org

FURTHER READING

Here are some additional publications that the *Creativity as a Career* authors recommend to you. They're organised according to the chapter topics:

PROLOGUE // The idea of success

* Huber, Richard M. *The American Idea of Success*. Pushcart Press, 1987.
* Arden, Paul. *It's Not How Good You Are, It's How Good You Want to Be*. Phaidon Press, 2003.

YOU //

CHARACTER //

* Dweck, Carol S. *Mindset: How You Can Fulfil Your Potential*. Robinson, 2012.
* Kleon, Austin. *Steal like an Artist: 10 Things Nobody Told You about Being Creative*. Workman Pub., Co., 2012.
* Mäki, Teemu. *Taiteen Tehtävä*. Into, 2017. (Finnish only)
* Potter, Andrew. *The Authenticity Hoax: How We Got Lost Finding Ourselves*. Harper/HarperCollins, 2010.

ATTITUDE //

* Eastaway, Robert. *Out of the Box: 101 Ideas for Thinking Creatively*. Duncan Baird, 2007.
* Goleman, Daniel, et al. *The Creative Spirit*. Plume, 1993.
* Kessels, Erik. *Failed It!: How to Turn Mistakes into Ideas and Other Advice for Successfully Screwing Up*. Phaidon Press, 2017.
* Remvall, Ingrid. *Idésmart*. Fri Tanke Förlag, 2016. (Swedish only)

COMMITMENT //

* Allen, David. *Getting Things Done: The Art of Stress-Free Productivity*. Penguin Books, 2015.
* Csikszentmihalyi, Mihaly. *Good Business: Leadership, Flow, and the Making of Meaning*. Coronet Books, 2004.
* Litt, Toby. *I Play the Drums in a Band Called Okay*. Hamish Hamilton, 2009.
* Pink, Daniel H. *Drive: The Surprising Truth About What Motivates Us*. Riverhead Books, 2012.

REACH OUT //

- Currey, Mason. *Daily Rituals: How Artists Work*. Alfred A. Knopf, 2016.
- Heath, Chip and Dan. *Made to Stick: Why Some Ideas Take Hold and Others Come Unstuck*. Random House Books, 2010.

THE WORLD //

STAKEHOLDERS //

- Lois, George. *Damn Good Advice (For People With Talent!)*. Phaidon Press, 2012.
- Gladwell, Malcolm. *The Tipping Point: How Little Things Can Make a Big Difference*. Little, Brown and Company, 2006.
- Quicksprout. "The Complete Guide to Building Your Personal Brand." (Online) quicksprout.com/the-complete-guide-to-building-your-personal-brand/

PROMOTION //

- Keen, Andrew. *The Cult of the Amateur: How Today's Internet Is Killing Our Culture*. Currency, 2007.
- Ries, Al and Laura. *The 22 Immutable Laws of Branding*. HarperBusiness, 2002.
- Johansson, Tanja & Luonila, Mervi. *Making Sense of Arts Management: Research, Cases and Practices*. Taideyliopisto, 2017

MONEY //

- Allen, Nikolas. *Death to the Starving Artist: Art Marketing Strategies for a Killer Creative Career*. CreateSpace Independent Publishing Platform, 2013.
- Andalucía Emprende. "Development of Business Ideas and Models." Fundación Pública Andaluza, 2015. (Online, Spanish only) www.andaluciaemprende.es/herramientas-de-gestion/desarrollo-de-ideas-de-negocio/
- Congdon, Lisa, et al. *Art, Inc.: The Essential Guide for Building Your Career as an Artist*. Chronicle Books, 2014.
- Saatchi, Charles. *My Name Is Charles Saatchi and I'm an Artoholic*. Phaidon Press, 2009.
- Österåker, Maria. *Ta Betalt! Om Prissättning i Skapande Branscher*. Liber, 2010. (Swedish Only)

SECURITY //

- Boon, Marcus. *In Praise of Copying*. Harvard University Press, 2013.
- Boyle, James. *The Public Domain: Enclosing the Commons of the Mind*. Yale University Press, 2010.
- KitCaixa. "Young Entrepreneurs You Never Know What You Are Capable of until You Try." Kitcaixa Jovenes Emprendedores Online, www.educaixa.com/kitcaixa-jovenes-emprendedores-online

CRED ITS ART

entrepreneurial learning

This field guide and accompanying cards are products of El-Art 2.0, a strategic partnership project between art schools in Europe. The collaborating partners are: Escuela de Arte de Sevilla (Spain), Malmö latinskola (Sweden), Minerva Academie voor Popcultuur (The Netherlands), Noorderpoort School voor de kunsten KTM (The Netherlands), St Gabriel (Spain). The coordinating partner is Yrkesakademin i Österbotten (Finland).

El-Art (Entrepreneurial Learning for Artists) is set up to help integrate entrepreneurship in European art schools through the development and distribution of teaching material and training programs for teachers and students. The aim of the programme is to help art schools give their students the entrepreneurial skills necessary to thrive before they enter the working arena. The material in this field guide is also suitable for starting creatives who are looking to strengthen their entrepreneurial skills.

The El-Art program and this production are made possible with the support of the Erasmus+ programme of the European Union.

To learn more about the project and get in touch, visit el-art.org.

Co-funded by the
Erasmus+ Programme
of the European Union

This project has been funded with support from the European Commission. The European Commission support for the production of this publication does not constitute endorsement of the contents which reflect the views only of the authors, and the Commission cannot be held responsible for any use which may be made of the information contained therein.

EL-ART 2.0 CREDITS

Initiator and Project Manager
Rebecca Simons

Project Coordinators
Yrkesakademin i Österbotten: Linda Wester & Susanna Vestling

Project Economist
Yrkesakademin i Österbotten: Lis-Helen Ekman

Advising Partner & Project Trainers
Minerva Academie voor Popcultuur (The Netherlands): Roger Muskee & Rutger Middendorp

Project Participants
Escuela de Arte de Sevilla (Spain): Ainhoa Martín Emparan, Isabel Gutiérrez, Juan Jose Garcia-Navas, Mariano Velamazán Martínez; Malmö latinskola (Sweden): Emma Denward, Lena Ansner, Malin Brandqvist; Noorderpoort school voor de kunsten KTM (The Netherlands): Albert Westerhoff, Colien Langerwerf, Marieke De Vries-Voorzee; St Gabriel (Spain); Alberto B. Alonso, Eva L. Roncero; Yrkesakademin i Österbotten (Finland): Bo Forsander, Kaj Ahlsved, Maria Westerlund.

PUBLICATION CREDITS

Author
Rutger Middendorp

Text Editor
Katherine Oktober Matthews

Illustrations
Colien Langerwerf

Content Contribution and Interviews
Ainhoa Martín Emparan, Albert Westerhoff, Bo Forsander, Colien Langerwerf, Emma Denward, Isabel Gutiérrez, Kaj Ahlsved, Katherine Oktober Matthews, Lena Ansner, Malin Brandqvist, Maria Westerlund, Mariano Velamazán Martínez, Marieke De Vries-Voorzee, Rebecca Simons, Roger Muskee.

Expert Input and Interviewees

Adriana Santos (Spain); Albert Sunyer (Spain); Anna-Maria Helsing (Finland); Anya Janssen (The Netherlands); Caroline Leander (Sweden); CT Heida (The Netherlands); Donald Weber (Canada); Francisco Alcantara (Spain); Harma Heikens (The Netherlands); Highway Design (Finland); Iris Sikking (The Netherlands); Javier Medina (Spain); Jesús Prudencio (Spain); Jonas Liveröd (Sweden); Jose Chamorro (Spain); Karin Noeken (The Netherlands); Kathrine Windfeld (Denmark); Lars Embäck (Sweden); Leyp (The Netherlands); Maggi Olin (Sweden); Mara León (Spain); Marlies Dekkers (The Netherlands); Martin Brandqvist (Sweden); Maud van der Leeuw (The Netherlands); Melissa Henderson (Sweden); Memento Photography (Finland); Mercedes Eirín (Spain); Milla Edén (Finland), Nighon (Finland); Reinout Douma (The Netherlands); Roland Jonker (The Netherlands); Sebastian Fagerlund (Finland); Pelle Öhlund (Sweden); Peter Johansson (Sweden); Pilar Albarracin (Spain); Salvatore Vitale (Switzerland); Sema D'Acosta (Spain); Tobias Granbacka (Finland); UPTA (Spain); Victor Sågfors (Finland); Yukiko Kitahara (Japan/ Spain).

Visual Identity and Design
Nick Kailola

Online Development
Mariano Velamazán Martínez

Translations Spanish
Saint Gabriel International Center

Publisher
House of Oktober
Amsterdam, 2018

ISBN 9789493075009